MW01258004

# Harley-Davidson Motorcycles

1918-78

HARLEY-
DAVIDSON
PACKAGE TRUCKS
The Davidson JR's

# HARLEY-DAVIDSON Motorcycles

## Singles and Twins

## 1918-78

A Documentation by Halwart Schrader and Klaus Vollmar

1469 Morstein Road, West Chester, Pennsylvania 19380

This volume of the Schiffer Automotive Series is dedicated to the motorcycles of the American marque of Harley-Davidson. It is documented that in 1918, three days before the Armistice, the first American soldier crossed the German border (unknowingly) on a Harley — and this is where our look backward at facsimiles begins, continuing to the year 1978. We have sought not only American sales literature, in order to show the international character of this great marque, for even today, in the ninth decade of its existence, Harley-Davidson ranks among the prominent motorcycle manufacturers of the world. Thanks to the WK Verlag of Bad Salzuflen, from whom we obtained a great number of interesting materials that are published in this volume.

Halwart Schrader
Editor

Translated from the German by Dr. Edward Force,
Central Connecticut State University.


Library of Congress Catalog Number: 90-61748.



Printed in the United States of America.
ISBN: 0-88740-265-8

This book originally published under the title,
*Harley-Davidson, Singles und Twins Motorräder 1918-78,*
by Schrader Verlag GmbH, Hösseringen,
© 1990. ISBN: 3-922617-61-1.

Walter Davidson, 1908

# Contents

# The Wonder from Milwaukee

The history of the world-famous motorcycle marque of Harley-Davidson began in 1901 in a small wooden shed, where William S. Harley and his friend Walter Davidson put together their first motorcycle. The Davidson brothers William and Arthur were also present on that first day. All of them had very different jobs, but soon gave them up after motorcycle building had outgrown its amateur status. During the course of 1902 the motor developed by the young team grew to be ready for production, as did the frame — the basis was created.

The Harley-Davidson firm was officially founded in 1903. At first their motorcycles had one-cylinder motors and belt drives — as did all motorcycles at that time. But production proceeded only slowly — in 1903 no more than three cycles were built! There were just as many the following year, and in 1905 there were all of seven.

By 1907, though, the business had grown to the extent that justified its being turned into a stock company and moved into a larger building with 700 square meters of space. Milwaukee had become a motorcycle city! A total of seventeen employees worked for the new firm, which now produced 150 motorcycles a year. But the new building, as often happened in the USA at that time, was just a structure of wood and tar paper, and so it is no surprise that, just before the building was finished, the whole staff picked it up and moved it half a meter. This was necessary because the railway inspectors found that the new workshop was a little too close to the tracks of the Milwaukee Railroad and the proper margin of safety had not been maintained.

The proud motorcycle manufacturers of Milwaukee introduced their first V-Twin motor in 1909. This motor layout was to remain a typical pattern for the future. And they were generally large-volume, high-torque machines that were built under the HD name. What was most important, though, was the guarantee of quality. Scarcely another American motorcycle could compare with the Harley-Davidson in this respect. The very first machine, which was sold in 1903, was legendary for its long life — ten years later it was still covering twenty or more miles a day to the complete satisfaction of its owner, and had long since covered 100,000 miles.

**Right: A photo taken in 1916. At whom was the rifleman aiming?**

**Opposite page: Many Harley-Davidson advertisements do not lack an artist's signature.**

Another part of the Harley-Davidson image from the start was the constancy of its models. Very few changes were made over the course of the years, which meant that many older models could be repaired with newer parts. The comparatively great number of HD motorcycles from before 1939 that still exist today indicates the importance of their long life.

The real breakthrough, though, was not made by Messrs. Harley and Davidson until 1912. In that year they brought out a model that had an ohv motor as well as a clutch that was really trouble-free — a weakness of all motorcycles in those days. In 1913 every model could be bought with either chain or belt drive. Then the obligatory footboards were given a new function: they were used to activate a kick starter as well as the rear brake. As of 1915 all motorcycles were equipped with a three-speed transmission.

By this time the HD marque had gained a fine reputation. The U.S. Post Office equipped its country mail carriers with motorcycles of this brand — which meant an order for 4800 of them at one stroke. And Harley riders naturally took part in sporting events, usually with great success. National and international records were also set with HD cycles.

When the United States entered World War I early in 1917, Harley-Davidson was there. Thousands of their machines crossed the Atlantic. 1918 was the year in which many Europeans got their first look at an American motorcycle, and even dyed-in-the-wool patriots had to admit that the Harley was an excellent piece of work.

The first American soldier who reached the German border in the saddle of his Harley-Davidson was Corporal Roy Holtz of Chippewa Falls, Wisconsin. History also records the exact date: It was on November 8, three days before the Armistice. The American courier had not crossed the border deliberately, but by mistake.

The first HD to be produced exclusively with chain drive came on the market in 1920. At the same time, an electric system and a turning accelerator control were introduced. Front-wheel brakes were added in 1928.

There were constant improvements in details, but the basic design remained the same. The Harley with its thick tires, wide saddle and large-volume V-type motor never lost its characteristic

**This is the 750cc model of World War II vintage. It was produced in vast numbers for the US Army.**

**Right: A kind of birthday picture, taken in 1978 on the 75th anniversary of the Harley-Davidson firm.**

nature. Of course there were also models with flat (boxer) two-cylinder motors, including those made for the U.S. Army in World War II, and later there were singles like the 125 two-stroke of the early postwar days (DKW model), but the heavy 74 with the 1200cc motor and cowboy saddle was still the essence of the classic Harley.

In 1958 HD reached another milestone with the introduction of hydraulic brakes. The Hydra-Glide became the Duo-Glide a year later, with hydraulic shock absorbers; in 1965 the Electra-Glide appeared, with an electric starter. The Twin had attained 65 horsepower by this time.

By this time the Harley-Davidson name also stood for bicycles, golf carts with electric or gasoline engines, and three-wheeled delivery vehicles ("Servicars"). Like BMW in Germany, Harley-Davidson was the only American motorcycle manufacturer to survive the Japanese competition, and devoted fans all over the world assure the continued survival of the quality machines from Milwaukee to this day.

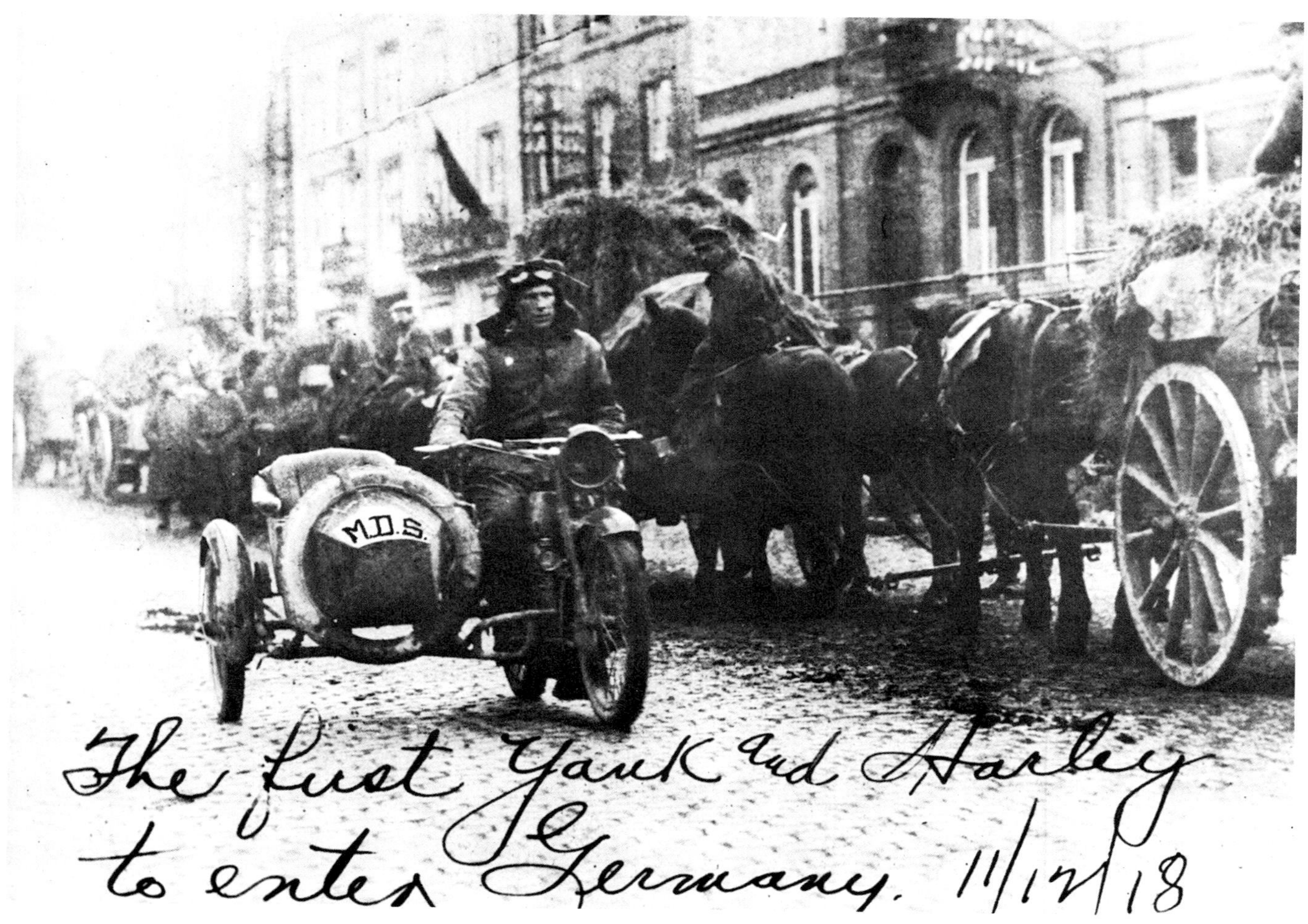
M.D.S.
The first Yank and Harley
to enter Germany. 11/12/18

This photo is a rare document in the factory archives. It shows the Harley rider Roy Holtz, the first US soldier who reached Germany at the end of 1918. A comrade-in-arms of the Corporal took the picture.

# Heavy Caliber

Motorcycle production in the USA, quite unlike that in Europe, had suffered no limitations during World War I, so that Harley-Davidson could justifiably call itself the "world's largest producer of motorcycles" at that time. The large-caliber models with 1000cc motors produced 16 horsepower, and the Milwaukee firm took pride in a list of 67 export countries. The advertising budget added up to a quarter-million dollars at that time, making Harley-Davidson one of the best media customers in the USA. And at a price of $310 in 1921, a Harley cost only $85 less than a *Tin Lizzie*, the lowest-priced version of which cost $395.

## The 3-Speed Twin Cylinder Models

THE three-speed twin is the most satisfactory all-purpose motorcycle. It is the logical touring machine—the logical sidecar machine—in fact, the logical machine for all-around general usefulness.

The Harley-Davidson was the first three-speed twin in America. This type has ever since been our leader and for this season 95 per cent of the Harley-Davidson production will be centered on the three-speed twin cylinder models 17-J and 17-F which fact furnishes the very strongest argument we can offer as to the popularity of this type.

The Harley-Davidson three-speed twin will go anywhere one cares to take it, over any public highway. Not only this, but it will take a sidecar and passenger over roads few other vehicles would care to tackle. It's a hill climber, a mud plugger; sand doesn't seem to phase it. On the hardest kind of cross country going the three-speed twin will take a sidecar with its passenger and luggage for thousands of miles and laugh at the task. In the most strenuous commercial service this type has shown that it is without an equal among horse drawn or motor vehicles.

For the rider who demands the very utmost in motorcycle engineering, we recommend the electrically equipped Harley-Davidson Model 17-J. This motorcycle is equipped with electric head light, tail light and warning signal. The convenience, neatness and compactness of the electrical equipment furnishes arguments enough to make the electrically equipped Harley-Davidson model the most popular machine we have ever manufactured.

The electrically equipped Model 17-J is offered as the finest example of motorcycle engineering the Harley-Davidson factories have been able to produce. Two years of use in the hands of thousands of Harley-Davidson riders in practically every civilized country in the world, have proven the electrical equipment to be extremely desirable.

*The electrically equipped 16-horsepower three-speed twin cylinder Model 17-J is shown on the front page of this folder. The 16-horsepower three-speed twin cylinder Model 17-F is illustrated on this page.*



**Right: The motorcycle industry used to be happy to publicize the number of speeds their models had. The 1918 Harley-Davidson had a three-speed transmission. Below: the 1918 prices.**

17-J Code Word—Fairy . . . . . . . . . $310
16 Horsepower, twin cylinder, 3-speed model with complete electrical equipment

17-F Code Word—Flower . . . . . . . . . $275
16 Horsepower, twin cylinder, 3-speed model

17-C Code Word—Fly . . . . . . . . . $240
6 Horsepower, single cylinder, 3-speed model

17-E Code Word—Flag . . . . . . . . . $255
16 Horsepower, twin cylinder, direct geared model

17-B Code Word—Fin . . . . . . . . . $215
6 Horsepower, single cylinder, direct geared model

17-L Code Word—Friend . . . . . . . . . $80
Standard pleasure sidecar

17-M Code Word—Flirt . . . . . . . . . $70
Sidevan with covered body 36¾″ long, 21¾″ wide, 18″ high in center and 15⅝″ high at the sides

17-N Code Word—Fig . . . . . . . . . $72
Sidevan with covered body 42″ long, 24″ wide and 18″ high

Harley-Davidson Motor Company
Milwaukee, Wisconsin, U. S. A.

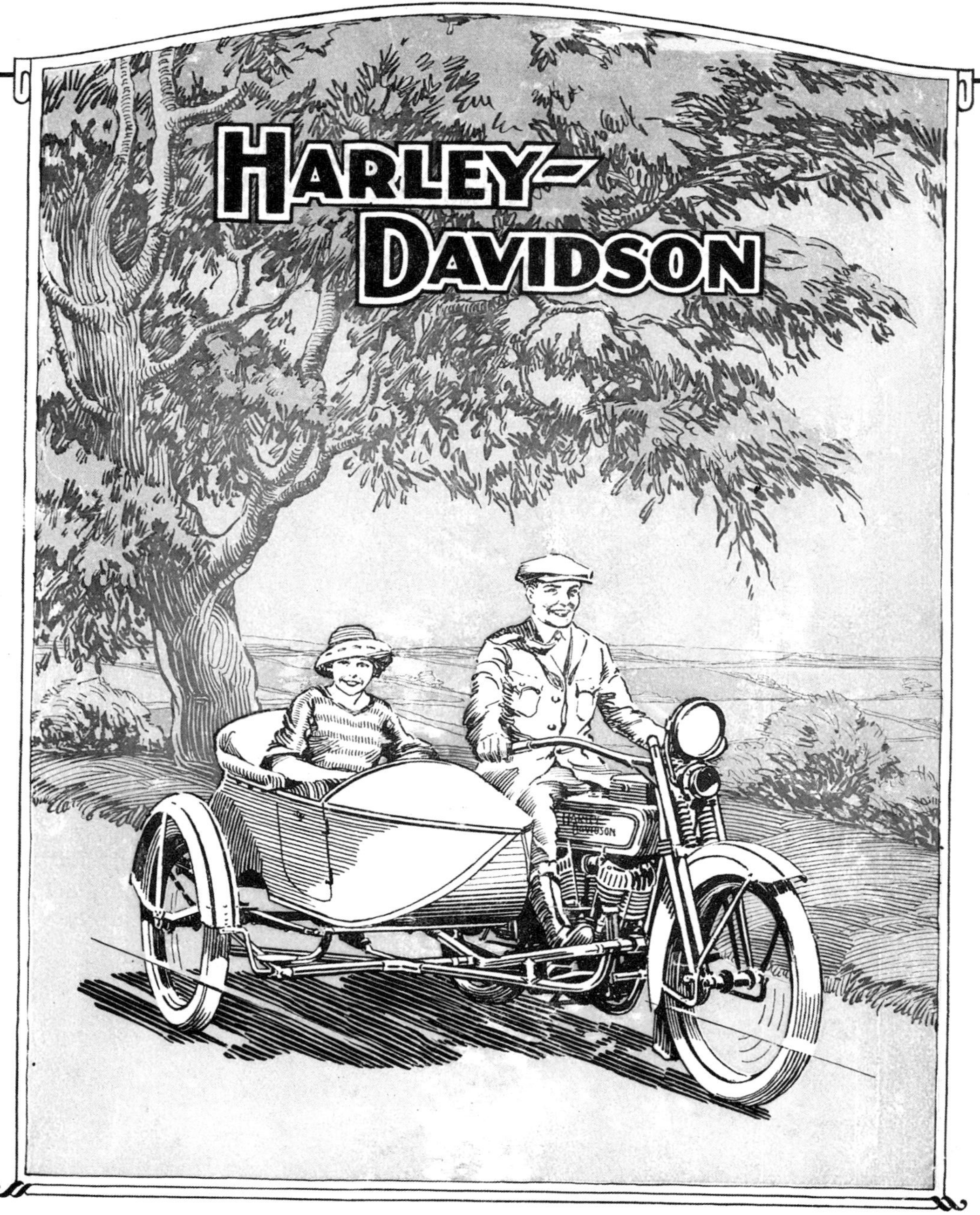


Title page of a 1924 catalog. The style corresponds to that used by the auto industry in the Twenties: line drawings in the sentimental manner.

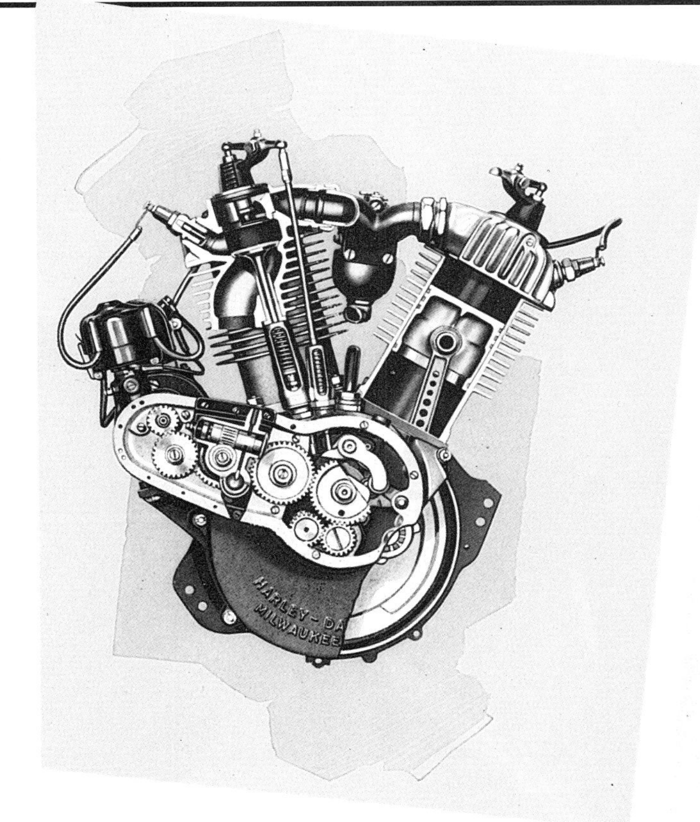


Above: The 1.2 liter motor of the big Harley-Davidson. With 87mm bore and 101.6mm stroke, the displacement was 1208cc. Right: A page from a catalog from The Netherlands. The larger models came with either magneto or battery ignition.

## HET 1924-1200 cM3 MAGNEET-MODEL

PORTSLUI, welke van solo-rijden en van de sensaties van snelrijden houden, alsmede zijspanrijders, die een reserve aan kracht wenschen, zijn enthousiaste aanhangers van het Harley-Davidson 1200 cM3 model.

De extra-zware machine bezit capaciteiten, welke het motorrijden tot de eerste buitenluchtsport op wielen maakt.

Lange, steile heuvels en snelrijden worden gemakkelijk gemaakt met deze krachtige machine. Voor het comfort bij het rijden is in ruime mate gezorgd.

Dit 1924 1200 cM3 model met magneet is bestemd voor rijders, welke magneet-ontsteking prefereeren. Deze machine wordt geleverd met carbid-koplamp, achterlamp, generateur en handclaxon. De ontsteking geschiedt door Boschmagneet.

Het electrische 1200 cM3 model is geïllustreerd op pag. 8 en 9. De uitrusting is dezelfde als het 1000 cM3 electrische model, doch heeft de eerste met den grooteren motor ook de grootere kracht.

In tegenstelling met de 1000 cM3 modellen, welke alle met aluminium-zuigers gemonteerd worden, kunnen de 1200 cM3 magneet- en electrische modellen zoowel met gegoten ijzeren als met aluminium-zuigers geleverd worden.

De wereld-reputatie der H. D. werd verworven met motoren, voorzien van gegoten zuigers, en worden deze in de 1200 cM3 klasse motoren nog aangeboden aan de rijders, die het verschil in prijs prefereeren boven verhoogde snelheid, kracht en optrekken, door motoren met aluminium-zuigers.

De magneet—zoowel als electrische modellen worden uitgerust met voorstandaard, bagagedrager, welke accessoires in onze prijzen begrepen zijn.

[11]

KÁLMÁN A. ARAD

# Modell 1925 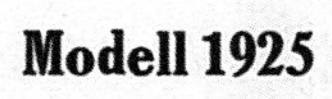  Preisliste 2403



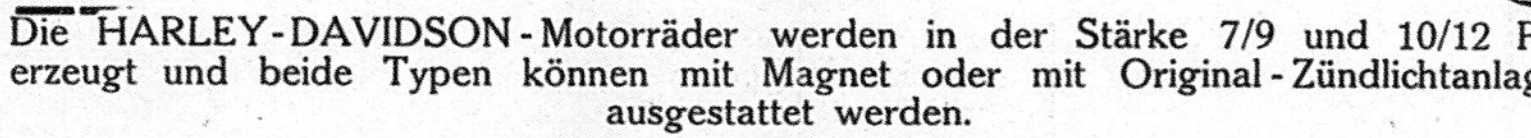

Die HARLEY-DAVIDSON-Motorräder werden in der Stärke 7/9 und 10/12 PS erzeugt und beide Typen können mit Magnet oder mit Original-Zündlichtanlage ausgestattet werden.

Nachstehend unser Preisanbot:

| MOTORRÄDER: | | | | SEITENWAGEN: | | |
|---|---|---|---|---|---|---|
| Modell | PS | Ausstattung | franko verzollt Wien | Modell | | franko verzollt Wien |
| M | 7/9 | Nr. 1 | S 3.600·— | E/1 | Prima englisches Fabrikat | S 1.200·— |
| D | 7/9 | Nr. 2 | „ 4.100·— | E/2 | detto für 2 Personen | „ 1.300·— |
| M | 10/12 | Nr. 1 | „ 3.900·— | A/1 | Orig. H.-D. Touring Luxusmodell | „ 1.700·— |
| D | 10/12 | Nr. 2 | „ 4.400·— | A/2 | detto extrastark für 2 Personen | „ 1.900·— |

**Chassis mit Kastenwagen je nach Ausführung.**

**Ausstattung Nr. 1**

Magnetzündung mit separater Lichtanlage (Azetylen oder elektrisch), 2 Bremsen, Tachometer (2 Zählwerke und Geschwindigkeitsmesser), Gepäckströger und komplettes Werkzeug samt Pumpe.

**Ausstattung Nr. 2**

Original HARLEY-DAVIDSON-Zündlichtanlage, bestehend aus Dynamo und Akkumulator (ersetzen sich im Störungsfalle gegenseitig), Stadtlicht, Scheinwerfer u. Schlußlicht samt elektr. Hupe u. Amperemeter. Sonstige Ausstattung wie Nr. 1.

**Alle Ersatzteile lagernd.**

**12 Monate Kredit! 2 Jahre Garantie!**

Neubauer, Wien, XII.

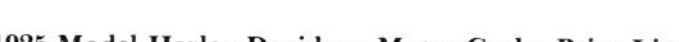

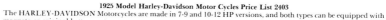

**1925 Model Harley-Davidson Motor Cycles Price List 2403**

The HARLEY-DAVIDSON Motorcycles are made in 7-9 and 10-12 HP versions, and both types can be equipped with magneto or original battery systems.

# 1200 c. c. Electric with Right Hand Sidecar

YOUR motorcycling joys will be doubled with one of these sidecars attached to your Harley-Davidson motorcycle. How often have you wished to take along a companion to share in the pleasures of your motorcycle jaunts and trips!

Riders and owners declare the Harley-Davidson sidecar is the easiest riding sidecar built. With its two 49 inch semi-elliptic springs, the sidecar passenger is floated over the bumps and rough spots in the road. Ask your dealer to give you a ride and you will get a surprise in easy riding comfort.

A snubber strap in front and an easily adjusted combination spring and snubber strap in the rear, check the rebound and add to the easy riding qualities of this sidecar.

All Harley-Davidson sidecars are regularly equipped with an adjustable axle at no extra charge. This permits a road tread of 44 to 56 inches. This is a feature greatly appreciated when covering rough, unimproved roads where it is necessary to follow wagon ruts. The axle is easily and quickly extended when road conditions require. The mudguard extends with the wheel and protects the sidecar passenger from being splashed by mud and water.

[8]

# The 1925—1000 c. c. Electric Model

THE popular 1000 c. c. Harley-Davidson model is offered for the 1925 season with a big array of improvements and refinements. The new low riding position will be quickly noticed. It is three inches lower than formerly. The rider can now put his feet firmly on the ground.

There is a new design frame that provides a low center of gravity and makes for a perfectly balanced machine. The drop forged head is extra strong and the loop of the frame is a wide trussed, crucible steel base that protects the bottom of the motor. There is the same liberal road clearance.

Much additional riding comfort has been built into the new models. The seat is extra large, form fitting. The cushion seat post is now fitted with a buffer spring and the main spring is fourteen inches long—five inches longer than formerly. The motor is fitted with lightweight iron alloy pistons. Three deep, narrow piston rings give long wear and hold compression.

This model is equipped with the reliable Harley-Davidson built single unit electric system. The ignition coil is now further protected with a metal cover. The battery is vertically mounted and easy to get at.

Electrical equipment on this model includes headlight, motor driven warning signal, generator, storage battery, manual ignition switch with warning alarm and tail light.

An ammeter, speedometer, additional heel brake, luggage carrier and front stand can be furnished if desired as extra equipment. This model, as illustrated on page 5, can also be obtained with Bosch magneto ignition.

[3]

**Left: Price list made for the Austrian market in 1925. The sidecar did not come from the USA. (Translator's note: E/1 and E/2 didn't, at least, though A/1 and A/2 seem to; apparently E means English and A means American.)**

**Above: A 1925 brochure. Here too, the model with "electric" (battery) ignition and many innovations is stressed.**

The New 350 c.c.
25.000.000
The 350 c. c. Single Cylinder Electric
The 350 c. c. Single Cylinder Magneto
The New Harley-Davidson Single
HERE is just the motorcycle you often thought about and wanted — a single cylinder, easy to ride, low in price, cheap in upkeep. No trick to ride it. Even a novice can learn within a few minutes. Wonderful balance—easy to control and handle. It's an honest-to-goodness motorcycle with performance that thrills the old timers and delights beginners.
Speed! — over fifty and then some. A sturdy single, designed with the exacting thoroughness and built to the high quality standards characteristic of Harley-Davidson.
Single Features:
Four stroke cycle motor, 346 c. c. piston displacement, side by side valves.
Harley-Davidson generator — battery, ignition and lighting system on electric model.
Switch panel and relay cut-out on electric model.
Magneto model, Bosch equipped.
Standard Harley-Davidson spring seat post.
Three-speed progressive transmission.
Regulation Harley-Davidson footboards.
Wheelbase, 55 inches.
Petrol capacity three gallons; oil three quarts.
Balloon tires, 26x3.30 inches, regular equipment.
80-90 miles to the gallon of petrol.
The New
Harley-Davidson
350 c.c.


Always a good seller: The 350 Harley Single. But there were always sales problems in the world of motorcycles. Harley-Davidson advertised time payment plans since 1924.

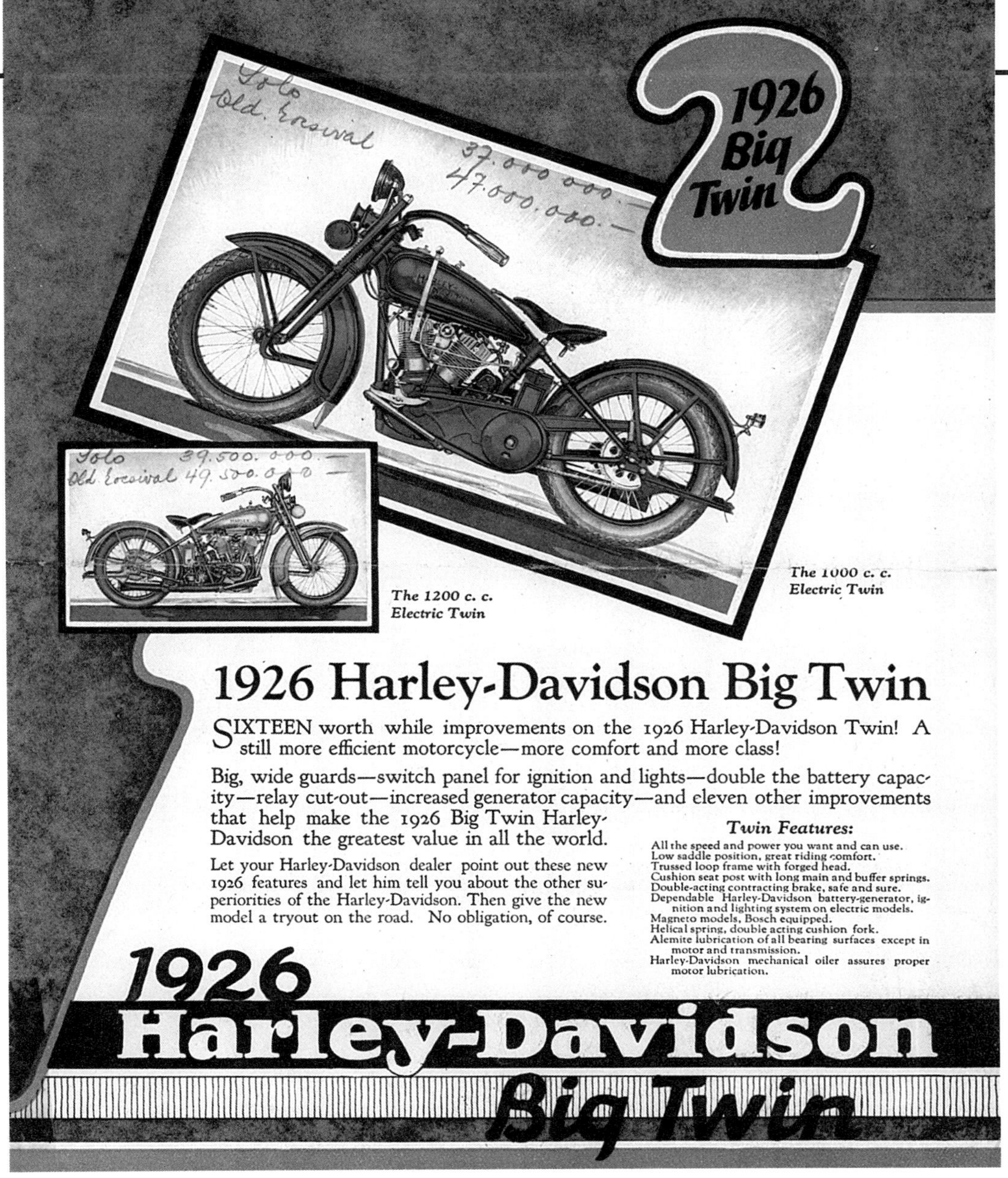


Big Twin, as the big machines were called — also called Models 61 and 74 (representing their displacement in cubic inches). For one's money one got "the greatest value in all the world," the ad said!

Geringere Spesen pro Kilometer!
Warum benutzen Sie einen Ein-Tonnen-Wagen um Ein-Pfund-Pakete zuzustellen?
Mit dem Harley-Davidson Liefer-Seitenwagen erledigen Sie die Anlieferung leichter Waren mit weniger als einem Drittel der Spesen, die Ihnen bei jeder anderen Transportart entstehen.
Beim Harley-Davidson Liefer-Gespann gibt es keine Verkehrsstockungen, keinen unnötigen Aufenthalt. Es ist denkbar leicht zu handhaben, zieht bei der geringsten Betätigung des Gasgriffes schnell an und windet sich leicht durch den dichtesten Verkehr, sodaß man die doppelte Anzahl Pakete in der halben Zeit eines Autos besorgen kann.
Das billigste und sparsamste Leicht-Liefer-Fahrzeug der Welt
und schnellere Lieferung

**This 1927 brochure appeared in German. The sidecar combination was improved again and again by Harley-Davidson to make business vehicles tasteful.**

**Lower cost per kilometer!**
**Why do you use a one-ton vehicle to deliver one-pound parcels?**

With the Harley-Davidson Delivery Sidecar you make the delivery of light goods cheaper, at less than one-third of what any other form of transportation costs.
With the Harley-Davidson delivery vehicle there are no traffic jams, no unnecessary delays. It is very easy to handle, accelerates quickly at the slightest touch of the gas control, and winds its way easily through the heaviest traffic, so that one can deliver twice as many packages in half the time a car takes.
The cheapest and thriftiest light delivery vehicle in the world and fast delivery

**The 1200 c.c. Two-seater**

No motorcycle of this type in all the world has come anywhere near equaling the popularity of the 1000 and 1200cc Harley-Davidson two-cylinder. These models are recognized everywhere as the epitome of motorcycle construction.

The 1200cc is the heavy model or oversize model and is preferred for trips with a sidecar, but also as a solo machine for those who value strong acceleration, particular power and speed. These qualities are represented in noteworthy fashion in this model.

Experienced motorcycle riders will attest that no motorcycle is built anywhere that lets one travel as comfortably as a Harley-Davidson. The big saddle, ideally formed, is supported by the famous Harley-Davidson cushioned seat post with springs that extend to the lower end of the frame. The springs — main, secondary and rear springs — bring the rider smoothly over bumps and ruts.

**The 1000cc Two-cylinder**

The 1000cc model is the popular two-cylinder machine for traveling with a sidecar as well as solo travel. High performance and speed are its outstanding characteristics.

The seat height on all Harley-Davidson motorcycles is notably low. At any time one can put both feet comfortably on the ground. Eight coil main and buffer springs in the front fork provide an effective suspension for all road conditions. The folding footboards are large and roomy. Tires are the full balloon 27 x 3.85 inch type.

The built-in ignition and lighting system is the well-known Harley-Davidson starter type. The ignition system is water- and weathertight. If you poured a bucket of water on the generator and distributor, it would not get in and cause the powerful spark to fail. The magneto models have a Bosch magneto.

**The 350cc One-cylinder with side valves**

This motorcycle has set new standards in the 350cc class. Pleasant and pretty to look at, it offers comfort such as has never been found in a model of this type before, which has won it particular popularity since it was introduced a year ago.

The same adjustable upholstered seat as on the two-cylinder type, low saddle position, folding footboards, ideally shaped saddle, double-acting coil main, rear and buffer springs on the front fork in combination with 26 x 3.3 inch full balloon tires provide highly pleasant driving. A single drive will convince you of the excellent evenness, light handling and riding comfort. Every Harley-Davidson dealer will be happy to give you the opportunity.

Great fuel economy is typical of this model. A consumption of 2.4 liters per 100 km on the average is reported by most drivers.

**The 350cc One-cylinder with overhead valves**

The solo rider who prefers a one-cylinder model with the greatest speed will be most keenly interested in this 350cc model with overhead valves. It is the same as the 350cc model depicted next to it, but with the difference that in this model the valves are located on the head.

Both 350cc models have the same three-speed transmission as the two-cylinder machine. Engine lubrication takes place via a directly working mechanical oil pump, assisted by an auxiliary hand pump. Nine bearing locations have fittings for high-pressure grease injection, which provides for easy lubrication.

The built-in Harley-Davidson ignition system provides strong headlight illumination, effective signal lights and water- and weather-tight ignition. Ignition and light switches can be covered and are located handily on a control panel behind the steering system. Magneto models have a Robert Bosch magneto.

Harley-Davidson — the most advantageous motorcycles and sidecars in the world!

## Der 1200 c. c. Zweizylinder

Kein Motorrad dieser Type hat in der ganzen Welt auch nur annährend die Popularität erreicht wie der 1000 und 1200 cc Harley-Davidson Zweizylinder. Überall werden diese Modelle als die Vollendung im Motorradbau anerkannt.

Der 1200 cc. ist das schwere Modell oder Übergrößenmodell und wird bevorzugt für Fahrten mit Seitenwagen, aber auch als Solomaschine für solche, welche auf starke Anzugskraft, besondere Kraftleistung und Geschwindigkeit Wert legen. Diese Eigenschaften sind an diesem Modell in bemerkenswerter Weise vertreten.

Geübte Motorradfahrer werden bestätigen, daß nirgendwo ein Motorrad gebaut wird, welches sich so bequem fahren läßt wie eine Harley-Davidson. Der große bestgeformte Sattel stützt sich auf den berühmten Harley-Davidson Kissensitzpfosten mit Federn, welche bis an das untere Rahmenende reichen. Die Federn — Haupt- Hilfs- und Rückschlagfeder — bringen den Fahrer über Höcker und Rinnen schwebend hinüber

## Der 1000 c. c. Zweizylinder

Das 1000 cc Modell ist die populäre Zweizylindermaschine für das Fahren mit Seitenwagen wie auch für Solofahrten. Hohe Leistung und Geschwindigkeit sind ihre hervorstechenden Merkmale.

Die Sitzhöhe an allen Harley-Davidson Maschinen ist überaus niedrig. Man kann jederzeit beide Füße bequem auf den Boden stellen. Acht schraubenförmige Haupt- und Pufferfedern in der vorderen Gabel bewirken eine wirksame Federung bei allen Wegeverhältnissen. Die klappbaren Fußbretter sind groß und geräumig. Reifen von Vollballontype 27×3,85 Zoll

Das eingebaute Zünd- und Lichtsystem ist die wohlbekannte Harley-Davidson Konstruktion vom Einleitertyp. Die Zündanlage ist wasser- und wetterfest. Man gieße einen Eimer Wasser auf Zündspule und Verteiler, und es wird nie ein Versagen des kräftigen Zündfunkens eintreten. Die Magnetmodelle haben Bosch-Magnet.

## Der 350 c. c. Einzylinder
### mit Seitenventile

Dieses Motorrad hat in der 350 c. c. Klasse neue Richtlinien aufgestellt. Gefällig und hübsch im Aussehen, besitzt es Merkmale der Bequemlichkeit, welche nie in einem Modell dieser Art vertreten waren, wodurch es sich eine besondere Gunst erwarb seit es vor einem Jahre herausgebracht wurde.

Derselbe einstellbare Kissen-Sitzpfosten wie am Zweizylinder, niedrige Sattellage, klappbare Fußbretter, bestgeformter Sattel, schraubenförmige doppelwirkende Haupt-, Rückschlag- und Pufferfedern an der Vordergabel in Verbindung mit Vollballonreifen 26×3,3 Zoll bewirken ein höchst angenehmes Fahren. Eine einzige Fahrt überzeugt von der großartigen Ausgeglichenheit, leichte Handhabung und Fahrbequemlichkeit. Jeder Harley-Davidson Vertreter wird hierzu gern Gelegenheit geben.

Große Brennstofferspamis ist ein Merkmal dieses Modells. Ein Verbrauch von 2,4 l pro 100 km im Durchschnitt wird von den meisten Fahrern berichtet.

## Der 350 c. c. Einzylinder
### mit Ventilen im Kopf

Derjenige Solofahrer, der eine Einzylindermaschine mit dem Höchstmaß von Geschwindigkeit vorzieht, wird für dieses 350 cc Modell mit Ventilen im Kopf das größte Interesse haben. Es ist dasselbe wie das nebenstehend abgebildete 350 cc Modell, nur mit dem Unterschied, daß bei diesem Modell die Ventile im Kopf angeordnet sind.

Beide 350 cc Modelle haben dieselbe Dreiganggetriebe-Konstruktion wie die Zweizylindermaschine. Die Motorschmierung erfolgt durch eine direktwirkende mechanische Oelpumpe, welche durch die Hilfshandpumpe ergänzt wird. Neun Lagerstellen haben Anschlüsse für die Hochdruck-Fettspritze, die leichte Schmierung gestatten.

Die eingebaute Harley-Davidson Einleiterlichtanlage gewährt kräftiges Scheinwerferlicht, wirksames Signal und wetter- und wasserfeste Zündung. Abschließbare Zünd- u. Lichtschalter sind bequem auf einem Armaturenbrett hinter dem Steuerkopf angeordnet. Magnetmodelle haben Robert Bosch Magnete.

**Harley-Davidson — die vorteilhaftesten Motorräder und Seitenwagen der Welt**

Another 1927 brochure in German. All the technical details are described in great detail. There was also a sidecar for two persons (side by side) offered by Harley-Davidson!

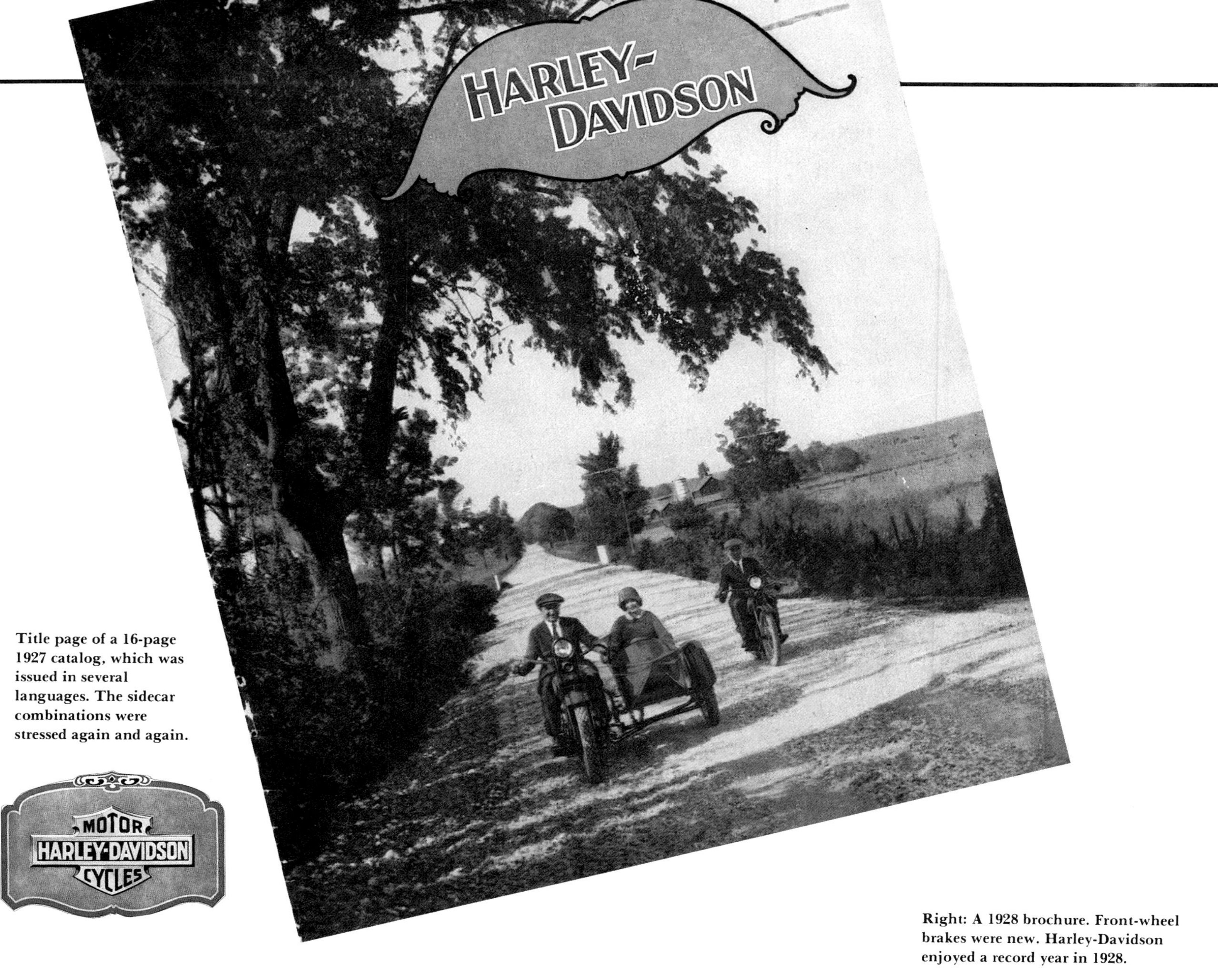


Title page of a 16-page 1927 catalog, which was issued in several languages. The sidecar combinations were stressed again and again.

Right: A 1928 brochure. Front-wheel brakes were new. Harley-Davidson enjoyed a record year in 1928.

**Main Improvements of the 1928 Models**

One of the greatest advances in motor lubrication in years was achieved by the introduction of oil provision regulated by the fuel throttle. Compared to the previous normal Harley-Davidson oil pump, the new system guarantees the direct supply of the right amount of oil for every engine speed. In the new model, the hand pump serves to rinse and refill the crankcase, This motor lubrication for all speeds is an essential factor in longer life and decreased maintenance costs.

The 1928 model Harley-Davidson now gives its drivers doubled security through the addition of a front-wheel brake, which effectively complements the rear-wheel brake. The brake on the front wheel is an internal shoe brake and works by expanding outward against the brake drum. It is activated by a very handy lever on the handlebars. The few individual parts are easily and directly adjustable. Both brakes give the rider absolute control over his machine at all times.

Among the characteristics of a modern motor is an air cleaner, which is available for all 1928 Harley-Davidson models. Harmful particles of dirt and dust are separated and held back by the air cleaner, so that they no longer pass through the carburetor into the motor. Carbon deposits as well as abrasion of surfaces working against each other are decreased, which also prolongs the motor's life.

One-cylinder machines with side valves, as well as two-cylinder machines with deluxe carburetors, are equipped with air cleaners.

## Hauptverbesserungen der Modelle 1928.

Neue Motorschmierung.

Eine der größten Fortschritte seit Jahren in der Motorschmierung wurde erzielt mit der Einführung der durch die Gasdrossel regulierten Ölzufuhr. Gegenüber der bisherigen normalen Harley-Davidson Ölpumpe wird bei der neuen Konstruktion nunmehr die direkte Zufuhr der für die jeweilige Motorgeschwindigkeit erforderlichen Ölmenge gewährleistet. Die Handpumpe dient beim neuen Modell zum Durchspülen und Neufüllen des Kurbelgehäuses. Diese Motorschmierung für alle Geschwindigkeiten ist ein wesentlicher Faktor für größere Lebensdauer und verminderte Unterhaltungskosten.

Das Harley-Davidson Modell 1928 gibt seinem Fahrer nunmehr eine doppelte Sicherheit durch Einbau einer Vorderradbremse, welche die bisherige bewährte Hinterradbremse wirksam ergänzt. Die Bremse am Vorderrad ist eine Innenbandbremse und wirkt von innen ansdehnend auf die Bremstrommel. Sie wird durch einen sehr handlichen Hebel an der Lenkstange betätigt. Die wenigen Einzelteile sind leicht und direkt nachstellbar. Beide Bremsen verschaffen dem Fahrer zu jeder Zeit die absolute Gewalt über seine Maschine.

Vorderradbremse.

Zu den Merkmalen eines Motors neuzeitlicher Bauart gehört ein Luftreiniger, der nunmehr für alle 1928er Harley-Davidson Maschinen erhältlich ist. Schädigende Staub- und Schmutzpartikel werden von dem Luftreiniger zurückgehalten und ausgeschieden, sodaß sie nicht mehr durch den Vergaser in den Motor gelangen. Kohle-Ablagerung sowie Abnutzung an aufeinander arbeitenden Flächen werden vermindert, wodurch auch die Lebensdauer erhöht wird.

Eincylinder Maschinen mit Seitenventilen sowie Zweicylinder Maschinen mit DeLuxe Vergaser sind m. Luftreiniger ausgerüstet.

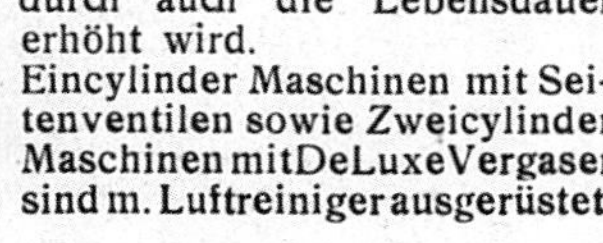

Luftreiniger.

### Technical Description

MOTOR — 1200cc, bore 86.97mm, stroke 101.60mm — 1000cc, bore 84.1mm, stroke 88.9mm — 750cc, bore 69.85mm, stroke 96.85mm — all side-valve four-stroke two-cylinder V-type motors — 350cc, bore 73.022mm, stroke 82.548mm, side- or overhead valve four-stroke one-cylinder.
CARBURETOR. Schebler de Luxe with air cleaner on all models.
LUBRICATION. Oil pump regulated by the accelerator handle on all models. Alemite nipples on all bearings.
IGNITION. Harley-Davidson generator and battery on all models.
GEARBOX. Harley-Davidson three-speed gearbox on all models.
ELECTRIC EQUIPMENT. Harley-Davidson generator, weathertight coil, battery, horn, two bull's-eye front lights, taillight, parking light, instrument panel with built-in ammeter on all models.
FRAME: Effectively strengthened seamless tube of high-quality carbon steel with reinforced joint piece. Steering head drop-forged.
BRAKES. Interior front, exterior rear heel brakes on all models.
CONTROLS. Turning handles, wires enclosed in handlebars and cables on all models.
DRIVE. Chain drive on all models.
SADDLE. Pan saddle on Harley-Davidson sprung seat post on all models.
TIRES: Balloon tires on all models.
WHEELBASE. 350cc 1.4 meters, 750cc 1.44 meters, 1000 and 1200cc 1.55 meters.
TANKS. Saddle type with oil container. Capacities for 350 and 750cc: 11.4 liters of fuel, 2.8 liters of oil; 1000 and 1200cc: 16, or 4.25 liter reserve tank.
FOOTBOARDS. Harley-Davidson type, folding up, on all models.
PAINT. Normal olive green paint.

## Technische Beschreibung

MOTOR — 1200 ccm, Bohrung 86,97 mm, Hub 101,60 mm — 1000 ccm, Bohrung 84,1 mm, Hub 88,9 mm — 750 ccm, Bohrung 69,85 mm, Hub 96,85 mm — sämtlich seitlich gesteuerte Viertakt-Zweizylinder-Motore vom V-Typ — 350 ccm, Bohrung 73,022 mm, Hub 82,548 mm, seitlich oder kopfgesteuerte Viertakt-Einzylinder.
VERGASER. Bei allen Modellen Schebler de Luxe mit Luftreiniger.
SCHMIERUNG. Bei allen Modellen vom Gasgriff aus regulierte Ölpumpe. Alemite-Nippel an allen Lagern.
ZÜNDUNG. Bei allen Modellen Harley-Davidson-Zündlichtmaschine und Batterie.
GETRIEBE. Bei allen Modellen Harley-Davidson-Drei-Gang-Schubgetriebe.
ELEKTRISCHE AUSRÜSTUNG. Bei allen Modellen Harley-Davidson-Zündlichtmaschine, wetterfeste Zündspule, Batterie, Horn, 2 Ochsenaugen-Frontlampen, Schlusslampe, Parklicht, Schaltbrett mit eingebautem Ampèremeter.
RAHMEN. Bei allen Modellen wirkungsvoll verstärktes nahtloses Rohr aus hochwertigem Kohlenstahl mit armiertem Verbindungsstück. Steuerkopf im Gesenk geschmiedet.
BREMSEN. Bei allen Modellen vorne Innen-, hinten Aussenbackenbremse.
BEDIENUNGSORGANE. Bei allen Modellen Drehgriffe. Drahtzüge im Lenker und in Kabeln eingeschlossen.
ANTRIEB. Bei allen Modellen Kettenantrieb.
SATTEL. Bei allen Modellen Pfannensattel auf Harley-Davidson-Feder-Sitzpfosten.
REIFEN. Bei allen Modellen Ballonreifen.
RADSTAND. 350 ccm 1,4 m, 750 ccm 1,44 m, 1000 und 1200 ccm 1,55 m.
TANKS. Satteltyp mit Ölbehälter. Fassungsvermögen 350 und 750 ccm, 11,4 l Brennstoff, 2,8 l Öl; 1000 u. 1200 ccm 16 bzw. 4¼ l Reservetank.
FUSSBRETTER. Bei allen Modellen Harley-Davidson-Ausführung, hochklappbar.
LACKIERUNG. Normale oliv-grüne Ausführung.

Harley-Davidson Motor-Company
Milwaukee, Wis. U. S. A.

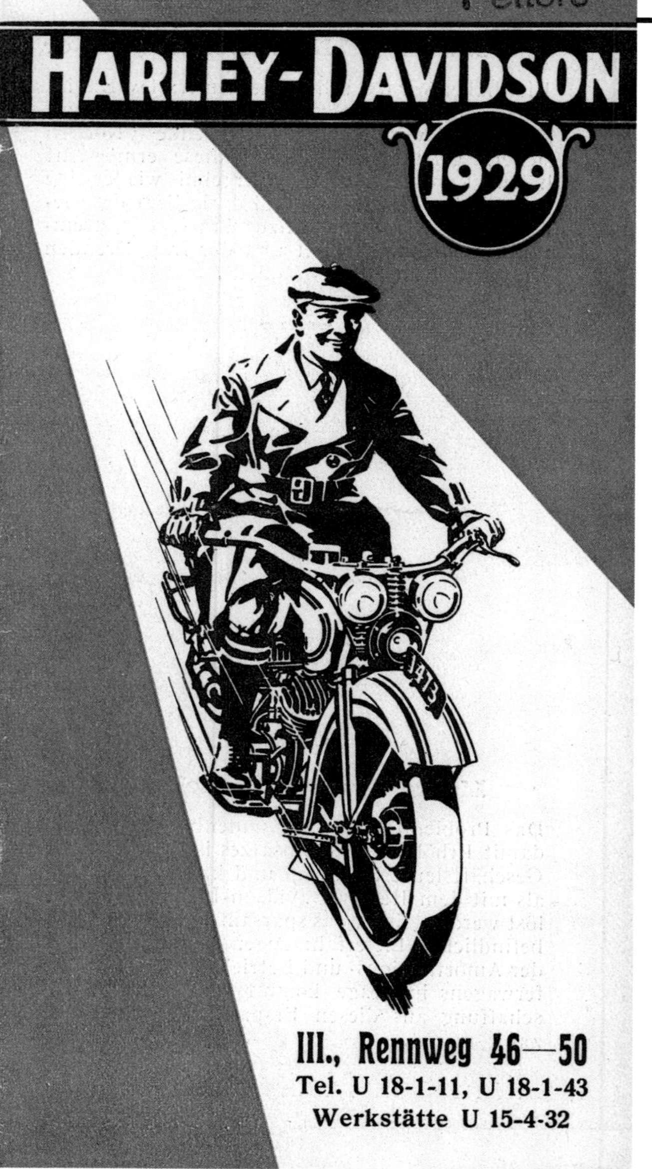

Petters
HARLEY-DAVIDSON
1929
III., Rennweg 46—50
Tel. U 18-1-11, U 18-1-43
Werkstätte U 15-4-32

**The prices include complete electrical equipment and double odometer.**
**New Features of the 1929 Model**

To the many outstanding features that have made Harley-Davidson the most popular motorcycle in the whole world, five more, of great importance, have been added on the 1929 model.
The two bull's-eye headlights give an improved light and heightened safety for night riding, and also contribute significantly to the low, neat lines of the 1929 models. With one simple switch on the right handlebar, the driver can make the light suit the road conditions at any time: two long, bright cones of light blending on the road surface, or one dimmed light for the city.
For further heightening of riding safety, the 1929 models have been fitted with a new, especially clear-sounding klaxon horn. This electrically operated horn has a particularly penetrating and yet pleasant tone and represents an important safety factor for fast driving. The new Harley-Davidson models have attained an extraordinarily effective dampening of noise through the introduction of the four-pipe exhaust system, without taking anything away from the power and speed. This brilliant design conducts the exhaust gases to either side of the rear wheel and provides ample service through the four slit pipes.
A further notable improvement is the new instrument panel, which includes the reliable Harley-Davidson-Weston ammeter, the switches for ignition and light, and a small shielded parking light, easy to see from front and back. In this tastefully formed and nicely made black enameled instrument panel, beauty and practicality are united in an ideal manner.
And finally, to bring perfection to its height, the electrical system has a regulator lever attached directly on the outside of the generator. This brilliant innovation puts the driver in a position to regulate the electric output and always to keep the battery fully charged according to the ammeter readings. Thus it is certainly one of the most useful and noteworthy features ever found on a motorcycle.

Die Preise gelten einschließlich kompletter elektrischer Ausstattung mit Doppelzählwerk-Tachometer

# Neuerungen des Modells 1929

**2 Ochsenaugen-Frontlampen**
— helleres und besseres Licht

**Stellhebel zum Regulieren der Dynamo-Stromstärke**
— von prompter Wirkung

**Vierröhriger Auspuff**
— völlig geräuschlos

**Helltönendes Signal**
— verschafft grössere Sicherheit

**Neuartiges Schaltbrett**
— mit Ampèremesser

**und eine Reihe weiterer wichtiger Verbesserungen.**

Zu den vielen hervorstechenden Eigenschaften, die Harley-Davidson in der ganzen Welt zum beliebtesten Motorrad gemacht haben, sind beim Modell 1929 fünf weitere von grosser Bedeutung hinzugekommen.

Die 2 Ochsenaugen-Frontlampen liefern ein verbessertes Licht und erhöhte Sicherheit bei Nachtfahrten, tragen dabei noch wesentlich zu dem niedrigen, schnittigen Aussehen der 1929er Modelle bei. Durch einen einfachen Hebelschalter an der rechten Lenkerseite kann der Fahrer jederzeit sein Licht den Strassenverhältnissen anpassen: zwei lange, helle, sich verschmelzende Lichtkegel auf der Landstrasse oder ein abgeblendetes Licht für die Stadt.

Zur weiteren Erhöhung der Fahrsicherheit werden die 1929er Modelle mit einem neuen besonders helltönenden Klaxon-Horn ausgerüstet. Dieses elektrisch angetriebene Horn hat einen besonders durchdringenden und doch angenehmen Ton und stellt bei sehr schnellem Fahren einen wichtigen Sicherheitsfaktor dar. Die neuen Harley-Davidson-Modelle haben durch die Einführung des vierröhrigen Auspuffs eine aussergewöhnlich wirkungsvolle Schalldämpfung erhalten, ohne dass der Kraft und Geschwindigkeit irgendwie Abbruch getan wird. Diese geniale Konstruktion leitet die Abgase zu beiden Seiten des Hinterrades und bietet durch die vier geschlitzten Rohre reichlichen Abzug.

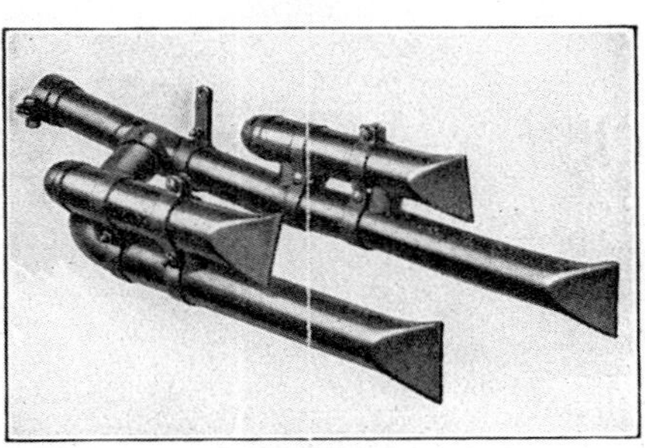

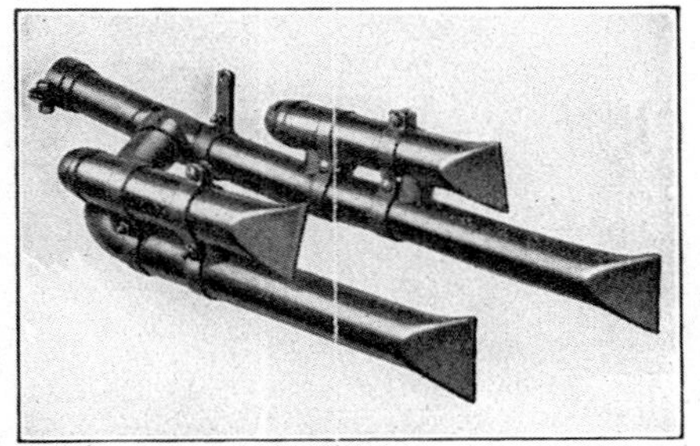

Eine weitere nennenswerte Verbesserung ist das neue Schaltbrett, in das der zuverlässige Harley-Davidson-Weston-Ampèremesser, die Schalter für Zündung und Licht und ein kleines geschütztes, von vorne wie hinten gut sichtbares Parklicht eingebaut sind. In diesem geschmackvoll geformten und hübsch ausgeführten schwarz emaillierten Schaltbrett sind Schönheit und Zweckmässigkeit in idealer Weise vereinigt.

Und um endlich die Vollkommenheit auf den Gipfel zu bringen, ist an der Zünd-Licht-Maschine ein Regulierhebel angebracht worden, der sich direkt auf der Aussenseite des Dynamo befindet. Diese geniale Neuerung versetzt den Fahrer in die Lage, die Strom-Erzeugung jederzeit zu regulieren und die Batterie nach den Ablesungen auf dem Ampèremesser immer voll geladen zu halten, ist also gewiss eine der nützlichsten und bemerkenswertesten Einrichtungen, die sich je an einem Motorrad befunden haben.

## New Models

A 45 cubic inch Twin (737cc) came on the market in 1929, naturally with the same technical details as the big Models 61 and 74. But dark clouds had come — the economic crisis was felt everywhere, and the motorcycle was not always the economical alternative to the automobile.

Many of the German importers have prominent names even today. Georg Suck of Hamburg was already one of them in the Twenties, as were Vise/ in Aachen and Haberl - now MAHAG — in Munich.

# Preise der Harley-Davidson Motorräder

Sämtliche Preise verstehen **sich frei Berlin und einschließlich folgender Ausstattung:** Elektrischer Beleuchtung, bestehend aus: Fern-, Stadt-, und Schlußlicht, Tachometer mit Beleuchtung, elektrischem Horn, Amperemesser, Gepäckhalter, Vorderradständer, Spezial-Werkzeug, Luftpumpe und Fettpresse sowie Ballonbereifung.

| | | | | |
|---|---|---|---|---|
| 1200 ccm Touren | 4,63 Steuer-PS. | 28 effektiv PS. | RM. | 2150.– |
| 1200 ccm Super Sport | 4,63 Steuer-PS. | 32 effektiv PS. | RM. | 2450.– |
| 1000 ccm Touren | 3,8 Steuer-PS. | 24 effektiv PS. | RM. | 2150.– |
| 750 ccm | 2,9 Steuer-PS. | 18 effektiv PS. | RM. | 1875.– |
| 500 ccm | 1,9 Steuer-PS. | 12 effektiv PS. | RM. | — — — |
| 350 ccm Touren | 1,3 Steuer-PS. | 7,5 effektiv PS. | RM. | 1550.– |
| 350 ccm Sport | 1,3 Steuer-PS. | 10 effektiv PS. | RM. | 1650.– |
| 350 ccm Super Sport | 1,3 Steuer-PS. | 13 effektiv PS. | RM. | 1700.– |

**Harley-Davidson Original Touren-Seitenwagen** ausgerüstet mit Patent Windschutz, Gepäckraste, Reifenhalter, Fußstütze und Seitenbeleuchtung . . . einsitzig RM. 850.–

**Derselbe** . . . zweisitzig RM. 950.

**Harley-Davidson Original-Seitenwagen** leicht . . . RM. 750.–

**Harley-Davidson Original Lieferwagen Chassi** . . . RM. 520.–

Aufbau für Lieferwagen nach Angabe unter billigster Preisberechnung.

**Günstige Abzahlungsbedingungen nach Übereinkunft.**

Diese Offerte versteht sich freibleibend.

## Importeure für Deutschland:

**R. W. Ott & Co.,** Berlin-Charlottenburg, Bismarckstr. 77, für Berlin und Brandenburg.
**Georg Suck,** Hamburg, Carolinenstr. 14, für Hamburg und Mecklenburg.
**Gustav Haferkorn,** Leipzig, Eutritzscher Str. 12, für Leipzig und Freistaat Sachsen.
**K. Haberl,** München, Isarthorplatz 2, für München und Bayern.
**Wenzel & Hibbeler,** Breslau I, Alte Taschenstr. 23/24 für Breslau und Schlesien.
**Friedrich Viesé & Co.,** Aachen, Frankenstr. 5, für Aachen und Rheinland.
**Hans Lutz,** Magdeburg, Walter Rathenaustr. 16, für Magdeburg und Provinz Sachsen.

Prices of Harley-Davidson Motorcycles

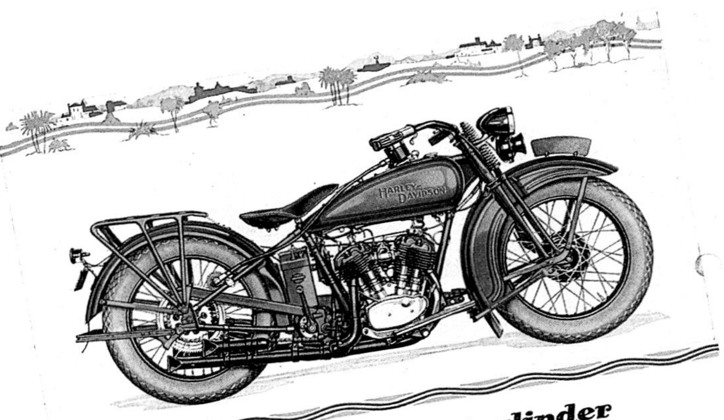


## Der 750 ccm Zweizylinder

Schnell wie der Wind, von vollendeter Schönheit, verläßlich wie ein alter treuer Freund, so ist der neue 750 ccm Zweizylinder, ein Meisterwerk der Technik von jedem Gesichtswinkel aus, an Aussehen, Konstruktion, Bequemlichkeit, Zuverlässigkeit wie Kraftentwicklung.

Er ist wunderbar leicht zu handhaben, schwebt über die Straße wie ein Windspie , liegt prachtvoll in den Kurven und nimmt spielend jede Steigung, ohne daß die Kraftreserve ganz beansprucht werden müßte. Ob es durch loses Geröll, tiefen Sand, durchfurchte Ackerwege oder über Asphalt geht, das macht für den Fahrer dieser ruhig und gleichmäßig laufenden Maschine nicht den geringsten Unterschied. Eine vollkommene Gewichtsverteilung mit sehr tiefer Schwerpunktslage und die niedrige Sattelstellung ermöglichen es dem Benutzer dieses neuen Typs, Tag für Tag ohne die geringste Ermüdung zu fahren.

Der Besitz eines solchen Fahrzeuges kann wirklich stolz und froh zugleich machen. Der seitlich gesteuerte Motor hat abnehmbare Original Ricardo Zylinderköpfe, die ein schnelles Entrußen und Einschleifen der Ventile gestatten. Kolben aus Magnesium-Metall bewirken die ruhige und gleichmäßige aber dennoch unwiderstehliche Kraftentfaltung bei jeder Geschwindigkeit. Breite vollkommen schützende Kotflügel, doppelte vordere Kette mit doppelten Kettenrädern und all die vielen anderen technischen Errungenschaften lassen erkennen, daß etwas auch nur annähernd so vollkommenes bisher in der Geschichte des Motorrades nicht bestanden hat.

*Der 750 ccm Zweizylinder, die ideale Solo-Maschine*

[4]

Speed and performance are promised by the title-page graphic art of this catalog, which came out in 1929. The big 1000 and 1200 models (61 and 74 cubic inches) had undergone improvements, and there was a new 750 (41 cubic inches), described at right.

**The 750cc Two-Cylinder**

Fast as the wind, of perfected beauty, reliable as a good old friend, this is the new 750cc two-cylinder, a masterpiece of technology from every standpoint, in appearance, design, comfort, reliability and production of power.

It is wonderfully easy to handle, sweeps over the road like a breeze, takes curves excellently and handles every upgrade playfully, without having to call on all its power reserves. Whether it is riding on loose gravel, deep sand, rutted farm paths or asphalt does not make the least bit of difference for the driver of this quietly and evenly running machine. An even weight distribution with a very low center of gravity and the low saddle position make it possible for the user of this new model to ride day after day without the slightest fatigue.

Owning such a motor vehicle can really make one proud and happy at the same time. The side-valve motor has removable original Ricardo cylinder heads that guarantee a quick cleaning and smoothing of the valves. Pistons of magnesium metal produce power quietly and evenly but undeniably at any speed. Wide, completely protective fenders, double front chains with double link wheels, and all the many other technical details let you know that something even approaching this perfection has never before existed in the history of the motorcycle.

Title page of a 1932 brochure.

Come in see the 1935 HARLEY-DAVIDSONS

★ Great advancements in the new models. Cam ground T-slot pistons—Honed, gun barrel finish cylinders—Demountable rear wheel and constant mesh transmission on the 45 Twin—Large filler caps—New air intake—Prefocused headlight—Five color options in new design—Many other features. Our demonstrators are here. Come in today and look over these greatest of all Harley-Davidsons.

Give 'em an "EAGLE EYE"!

**Visibility—Unobstructed View—Uninterrupted Vision!**

To the motorcycle officer, the boulevard ahead unfolds in an endless panorama. Side streets hold no secrets. No window frames to make him "lose" a car. No reason to rely on the "judgment" of a rear vision mirror . . . The motorcycle officer "sees all," and because he has full vision, he is a vitally important factor in traffic control — accident prevention — loss of life.

That's why we say —"give your traffic squad an eagle eye" — the latest Harley-Davidsons — with or without radios and sidecars. Sturdy, reliable, economical — the Harley-Davidson Police model has grown up with traffic control problems and is truly "The Police Motorcycle."

*Ask your Harley-Davidson Dealer or write us for complete details and special Police literature.*

HARLEY-DAVIDSON MOTOR CO.
Milwaukee, Wisconsin

HARLEY-DAVIDSON
*The Police Motorcycle*

**Advertisements dating from 1934, 1935 and 1939. In those years Harley-Davidson motorcycles were significantly modernized.**

HARLEY-DAVIDSON for 1939

● New beautiful tail light—Streamlined instrument panel—Two-tone russet rhino-grain horsehide saddle top—Self-aligning upper and lower head cones —Improved motor performance—New ride control on 45 Twin—Steel-strutted pistons on 74 and 80 Twins—New design 25-ball clutch push rod bearing on Big Twins—Stainless steel fender strips—New eye-appealing color scheme—New color options.

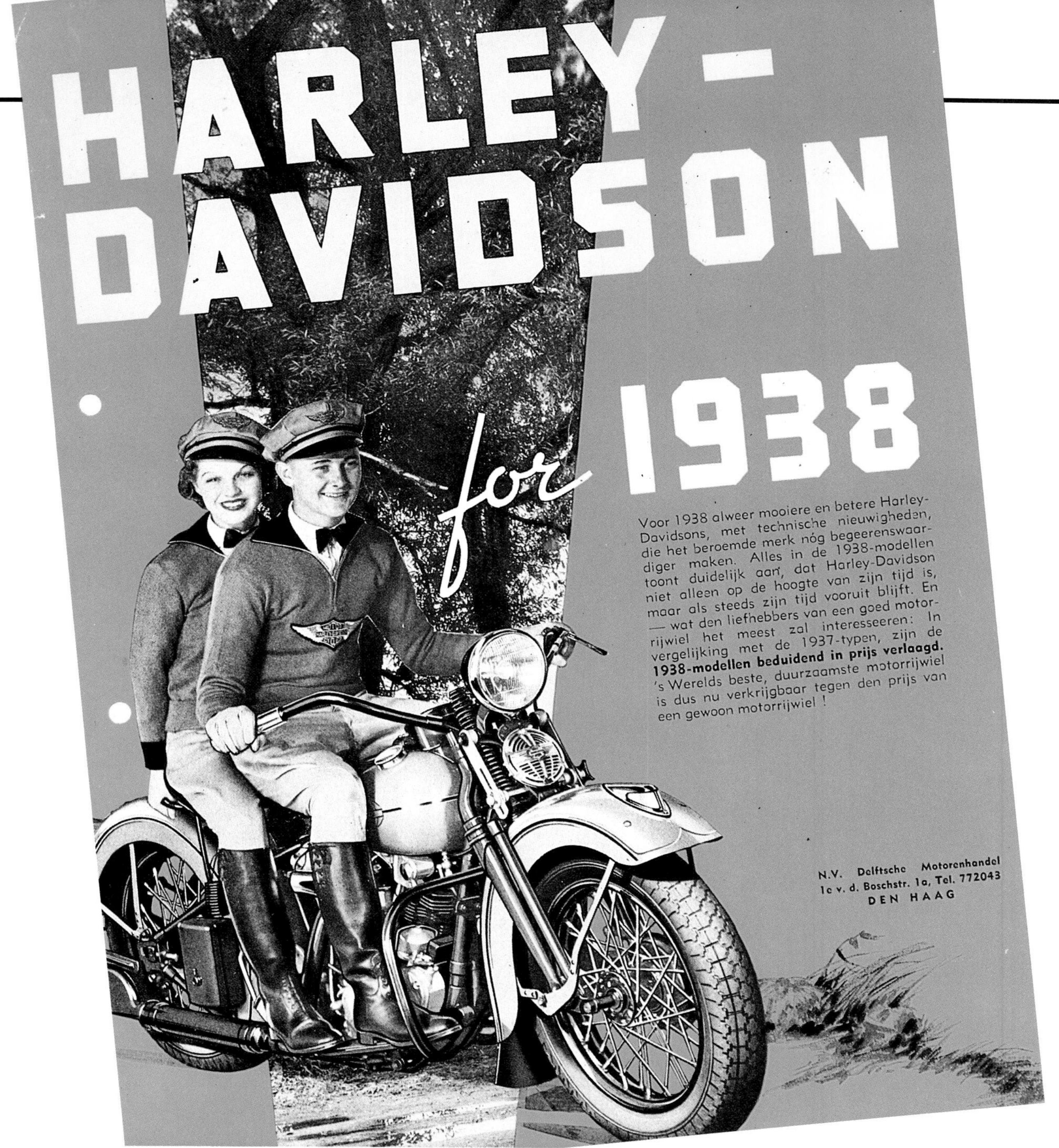
HARLEY-
DAVIDSON
for 1938
Voor 1938 alweer mooiere en betere Harley-
Davidsons, met technische nieuwigheden,
die het beroemde merk nóg begeerenswaar-
diger maken. Alles in de 1938-modellen
toont duidelijk aan, dat Harley-Davidson
niet alleen op de hoogte van zijn tijd is,
maar als steeds zijn tijd vooruit blijft. En
— wat den liefhebbers van een goed motorrijwiel het meest zal interesseeren: In
vergelijking met de 1937-typen, zijn de
1938-modellen beduidend in prijs verlaagd.
's Werelds beste, duurzaamste motorrijwiel
is dus nu verkrijgbaar tegen den prijs van
een gewoon motorrijwiel !
N.V. Delftsche Motorenhandel
1e v. d. Boschstr. 1a, Tel. 772043
DEN HAAG

**HARLEY-DAVIDSON FOR 1932**

**The greatest values in motorcycles that have ever been offered!**

Two new models, a newly designed 750cc two-cylinder and a completely new 350cc one-cylinder — many improvements to all models — new prices, the lowest in years — these are the high points of the series for 1932.

**1200cc Two-Cylinder**

As before, this wonderful large two-cylinder motorcycle leads the way in design and engineering art. Basically the same as the thousands on thousands of Harley-Davidson machines that have achieved such noteworthy success in all parts of the world, the new 1200cc for 1932 is an even finer and more capable motorcycle than them all. With its many new innovations and refinements, it is now more than ever the superb motorcycle. And yet the price of this great two-cylinder for 1932 has been lowered significantly.

**750cc Two-Cylinder**

This new 750cc for 1932 is the most excellent medium-strength two-cylinder machine that has ever been offered, and it wins the greatest respect from drivers everywhere. It is smaller and lighter than the big two-cylinder, but has more than enough power, lightning-fast acceleration, the greatest comfort, and is easy to handle. The 750cc motor has been newly designed for 1932, with smoother running, better lubrication, even greater reliability and an even longer life. Many of the innovations are identical to those of the large two-cylinder machine.

# HARLEY-DAVIDSON FUER 1932

## *—Die Grössten Werte in Motorrädern Die Je Angeboten Worden Sind!*

Zwei neue Modelle, ein neukonstruiertes 750 ccm Zweizylinder und ein ganz neues 350 ccm Einzylinder—viele Verbesserungen an allen Modellen—neue Preise, die niedrigsten in Jahren—dies sind die Glanzpunkte bei der Serie für 1932.

### 1200 ccm Zweizylinder

Wie bisher, leitet dieses wundervolle grosse Zweizylinder-Motorrad den Weg in Konstruktion und Ingenieurkunst. Grundsätzlich dieselbe wie die tausende über tausende von Harley-Davidson Maschinen die in allen Teilen der Welt solch bemerkenswerte Erfolge errungen haben, ist die neue 1200 ccm für 1932 ein noch feineres und leistungsfähigeres Motorrad als sie alle. Mit seinen vielen Neuerungen und Verfeinerungen ist es nun mehr als je das Motorrad superb. Und dazu noch ist der Preis dieser grossen Zweizylinder für 1932 bedeutend heruntergesetzt.

### 750 ccm Zweizylinder

Diese neue 750 ccm für 1932 ist die vortrefflichste mittelstarke Zweizylindermaschine, die je angeboten worden ist, und sie findet überall bei Fahrern den grössten Anklang. Dieselbe ist kleiner und leichter als die grosse Zweizylinder, hat aber reichlich genug Kraft, blitzartiges Anzugsvermögen, äussersten Komfort, und ist von leichter Handhabung. Der 750 ccm Motor ist für 1932 neukonstruiert worden um einen weicheren Gang, bessere Schmierung, noch grössere Zuverlässigkeit und eine noch längere Lebensdauer zu sichern. Viele der Neuerungen sind identisch mit denen an der grossen Zweizylindermaschine.

**Left: Title page of a brochure for Holland. The Harley cap was a status symbol in Europe too!**

**Above: One can tell by the German text that this brochure was also printed in the USA.**

# 10 Hervorragende Vorzuege Der Neuen Modelle 1932

Untenstehend sind zehn der wichtigeren Vorzüge der Harley-Davidson Modelle 1932 abgebildet. Ausser diesen haben diese wundervollen Motorräder hunderte von anderen Vorteilen in Konstruktion und Ausrüstung, welche für Harley-Davidson den Titel "Das beste Motorrad der Welt!" erworben haben.—Sprechen Sie heute bei Ihrem nächsten Harley-Davidson Vertreter vor, und lassen Sie sich die neuen Modelle ohne irgendwelche Verpflichtung Ihrerseits vorführen.

Schnellabnehmbare, auswechselbare Räder der 1200 ccm Zweizylinder. Es ist nur die Sache einiger Minuten, ein Rad zwecks Reifenauswechselung abzumontieren. Man brauch nur eine Mutter zu lösen, die Achse herauszuziehen, und das Rad kann herausgenommen werden, ohne die Bremsoder Ketten-Einstellungen irgendwie zu stören. Wann der hintere Reifen Abnutzung zeigt, brauch man nur die Räder auszuwechseln, und eine grössere Kilometerzahl pro Reifen wird erreicht. Tiefbettfelgen und Stahlseilreifen machen Reifenreparaturen zu einer Leichtigkeit.

Alle Harley-Davidson Modelle sind mit einer Duplex-Vorderantriebskette, die mit Doppelkettenrädern eingreift, versehen. Dieselbe wird vom Motor aus automatisch geschmiert und bedarf sehr wenig Wartung.

Alle Harley-Davidson Maschinen sind mit einer Vorderradbremse, die mittelst eines Hebels an der Lenkstange bequem betätigt werden kann, versehen. Eine Bremse ist auch an dem Beiwagenrad des grossen Zweizylindermodells vorgesehen.

Obenstehend ist die standhafte Hinterradbremse der 750 ccm Zweizylinder und der 500 ccm Einzylinder. Bei diesen Modellen hat die hintere Achse nun konische Rollenlager. Die Bremsverankerung und das Rad können jetzt viel leichter entfernt werden.

Für 1932 hat die 750 ccm Zweizylinder einen durchweg neuen Motor. Die Abbildung zeigt die rechte Seite, von welcher der Oelpumpenschutz entfernt ist. Man beachte die horizontale Lage des neuen Dynamos—gerade wie sie bei dem 1200 ccm Zweizylindermodell ist.

Alle Harley-Davidson Motoren haben abnehmbare Ricardo-Zylinderköpfe um grössere Kraft und leichtere Zugänglichkeit zu den Ventilen und Kolbenböden zu erzielen. Obenstehend ist der 500 ccm Motor, mit entferntem Zylinderkopf.

Der Vergaser der Zweizylindermodelle 1932 hat einige wichtige Neuerungen. Unter diesen sind ein Benzinsieb, ein verbessertes Schwimmerventil und ein langes, poliertes Lufteinlassrohr.

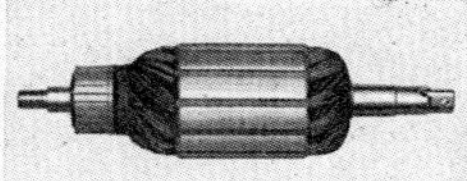

Die Zweizylindermodelle 1932 haben einen neuen Dynamo mit einem Kollektor von 24 Teilen und mit formgewundenem Anker. Die Lebensdauer der Bürsten ist verdreifacht worden.

Harley-Davidson Maschinen sind überall in der Welt für ihre erstaunlich grosse Fahrbequemlichkeit bekannt. Einer der Hauptvorzüge ist der exklusive, patentierte, gefederte Sitzpfosten. Aus der Abbildung ist ersichtlich wie die Spiralfedern den ganzen Weg herunter bis unten an den Rahmen gehen. Der Sattel ist auf 19 Zoll (.48 m) von Stahlfedern, die nach dem Gewicht des Fahrers eingestellt werden können, montiert. Andere Dinge die zum Komfort beitragen, sind Vollballon-Reifen, Federgabeln, niedrige Sattellage, formgemässer Sattel, und grosse Fussbretter.

Der Burgess-Auspuff, der ausschliesslich bei Harley-Davidson Zweizylindermaschinen verwendet wird, ist ein wirksamer Schalldämpfer, der keine Zwischenwandungen hat und demzufolge kein Rückschlagen verursacht.

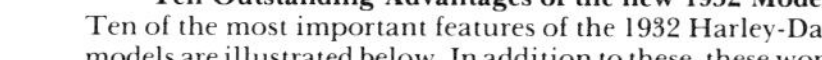

**Ten Outstanding Advantages of the new 1932 Models**

Ten of the most important features of the 1932 Harley-Davidson models are illustrated below. In addition to these, these wonderful motorcycles have hundreds of other advantages in design and equipment that have won Harley-Davidson the title of "the best motorcycle in the world!" — Talk to your nearby Harley-Davidson dealer today and see the new models without any obligation on your part.

Quickly removable, changeable wheels of the 1200cc two-cylinder model. It only takes a few minutes to remove a wheel for the purpose of changing a tire. One need only loosen a nut to pull out the axle and the wheel can be taken out without disturbing the brake or chain systems in any way. When the rear tire shows wear, one need only switch the wheels to attain a greater number of kilometers covered per tire. Deep-bed wheels and steel-belted tires make repairing a tire easy.

All Harley-Davidson models are fitted with a duplex front drive chain, which works with double-chain wheels. This is automatically lubricated from the motor and requires very little maintenance.

All Harley-Davidson machines are equipped with a front-wheel brake easily activated by a lever on the handlebars. There is also a brake on the sidecar wheel of the big two-cylinder model.

The picture above shows the sturdy rear-wheel brake of the 750cc two-cylinder and the 500cc one-cylinder. In these models the rear axle has only conical roller bearings. The brake attachment and the wheel can now be removed much more easily.

For 1932 the 750cc two-cylinder has a completely new motor. The picture shows the right side, from which the oil-pump protector has been removed. Note the horizontal position of the new generator — just as it is on the 1200cc two-cylinder model.

All Harley-Davidson motors have removable Ricardo cylinder heads to produce greater power and afford easier access to the valves and pistons. Shown above is the 500cc motor with its cylinder head removed.

The carburetor of the 1932 two-cylinder motor has several important innovations. Among them are a fuel strainer, an improved float valve and a long polished air intake pipe.

The 1932 two-cylinder models have a new generator with a 24-part collector with a wound-to-shape armature. This increases the life of the brushes threefold.

Harley-Davidson machines are known all over the world for their remarkably great riding comfort. One of the main advantages is the exclusive, patented sprung seat post. From the illustration it can be seen that the coil springs extend all the way down to the frame. The saddle is mounted at 19 inches (.48 meter) on steel springs that can be adjusted to the weight of the rider. Other features that contribute to the comfort are full balloon tires, sprung forks, low seat position, a shaped seat and large footboards.

The Burgess exhaust system, which is used exclusively on Harley-Davidson two-cylinder machines, is an effective muffler which has no intermediate walls and thus causes no backfiring.

The information in the 1932 brochure goes very much into detail. This is the back of the catalog whose title page is shown on page 26. The standard Harley colors are still olive with bright red stripes.

1933 **HARLEY-DAVIDSON**

Het beste is altijd het goedkoopste

VOLLEDIGE CATALOGUS, waarin de machines in de origineele kleuren zijn weergegeven, wordt op aanvrage franco toegezonden

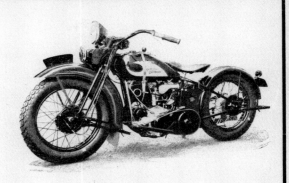

VOOR 1933 DE VOLGENDE TYPEN:

Één cylinders

Model B. 350 c.c., de goedkoope één cylinder voor alle doeleinden, speciaal voor bedrijf.

Model CB. 500 c.c., de laagst geprijsde één cylinder voor groote afstanden en met langen levensduur.

Model C. 500 c.c., de onverwoestbare één cylinder, ook te bezigen met zijspan

Twéé cylinders

Model R. 750 c.c., het toppunt van soeplesse met ongeëvenaard soepelen, snellen motor.

Model R.L.D. 750 c.c., de droom van den snelheidsliefhebber.

Model V. 1200 c.c., een meesterstuk van techniek m. groote krachtreseve.

Model V.L.D. 1200 c.c.... de onbereikbare snelheidsduivel.

HIERLANGS AFKNIPPEN

Ondergeteekende:

Naam:

Plaats:

Straat:

verzoekt zonder verplichting zijnerzijds toezending van

den Geïllustreerden Catalogus der

Harley-Davidson-modellen

Advertising with beauty and quality — but the times were not easy. Even the new half-liter machines are hard to sell. In 1933 HD sold no more than 6000 motorcycles.

Schoonheid
....gepaard aan Kwaliteit
Vijf schitterende kleurencombinaties zonder prijsverhooging
Bliksemsnelle - onvergelijkelijk soepele - comfortable
Twee Cylinders
Duurzame - bedrijfszekere - onverwoestbare
Eén Cylinders
Harley-Davidson
het kenmerk van Degelijkheid

# ANNOUNCING Servi-Car Service

Free Pick-up and Delivery Service for Your Car When It Needs Attention

CALL

[ PHONE NO. ]

WHEN your car needs service—repairs, adjustments, washing, greasing, oil changing, or whatever it may be—simply 'phone us and our Servi-Car driver will call for your car in a jiffy. When the work is finished he will deliver your car anywhere you wish. There is absolutely no extra charge for this wonderfully convenient service. Saves time and trouble and leaves you free to fulfill social or business engagements. Places our Service Department as close to you as the nearest telephone!

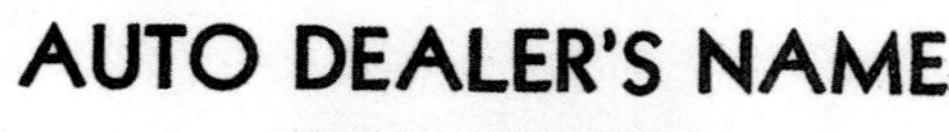

AUTO DEALER'S NAME
STREET ADDRESS
CITY AND STATE


## A Truck on Three Wheels

HD came on the market in 1931 with an interesting new design. This was the three-wheeled Servicar, a combination of motorcycle and delivery truck, which won great popularity, including with the police. Sales were associated with GM's Cadillac branch, an excellent combination.

SERVI-CAR PICK-UPS

No. 622

February 1, 1932.

COMMERCIAL SERVI-CARS NOW READY FOR DELIVERY!

Illustrated below is the Harley-Davidson Servi-Car with the Commercial Type body. The demand for a Servi-Car with larger carrying capacity for use in other lines of business was so great, that our engineering department developed this commercial model.

The specifications for this commercial type Servi-Car are identically the same as for the Servi-Car designed for the automobile field, except for weight and dimensions of the box. The Commercial Servi-Car, or model GD weighs 645 pounds and the dimensions of the body are as follows:

34-3/4 inches wide; 27-3/8 inches long, 16-1/2 inches high without cover.

The above dimensions give this type body a cubic foot capacity of 9 feet

SERVI-CAR WITH COMMERCIAL TYPE BODY

CADILLAC MOTOR CAR CO.
MILWAUKEE
BRANCH
Inaugurates
A New
Convenient
Time Saving
Residential Service
1707 EAST NORTH AVENUE
PHONE LAKESIDE 4870


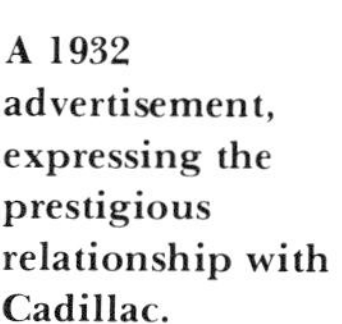
A 1932 advertisement, expressing the prestigious relationship with Cadillac.

**DE 61 – 1000 c.c. TWEE-CYLINDER**

De beroemde „knaap" onder de Harley-Davidsons. Een
snelheid, die sensationeel is, niets vóór zich behoeft te
dulden en die uren achtereen op peil blijft. Het was een
standaard 1000 c.c., waarop Fred. Ham zijn beroemde
24-uur-record vestigde, p.m. 3000 K.M. met een ge-
middelde snelheid van 125 K.M. per uur, een standaard
1000 c.c. waarmede Joe Petrali het Amerikaansche
record op 220 K.M. per uur bracht. Het ideaal van den
„echten" motorrot, die niet bang is voor een beetje
snelheid. Ook met een Harley-zijspan een ideale com-
binatie, die voor geen kleintje vervaard is. Getuigen de
6-daagsche in '36 en de talrijke successen op Duynrell.

**DE 45 – 750 c.c. TWEE-CYLINDER**

De populaire Harley-Davidson, die men bij honderden
op de Hollandsche wegen ziet en zich onder de motor-
rijders een groote schaar van vrienden heeft verworven.
Dat is te begrijpen, want de 750 c.c. paart een groote
souplesse aan een flinke snelheid, valt in den smaak
door gemakkelijke hanteerbaarheid en zuinigheid in
gebruik. Het is het ideale motorrijwiel voor den gemid-
delden motorrijder, die een aardige snelheid in zijn
machine wenscht, zonder dat dit ten koste gaat van
souplesse en voortdurende revisie. De 750 c.c. is in
verschillende uitvoeringen te leveren, voor hooge
en zéér groote snelheden.

**DE 74 – 1200 c.c. TWEE-CYLINDER**

De beroemde politie-motor, die in alle Nederlandsche
gemeenten van eenige beteekenis bijdraagt aan de
publieke veiligheid. Groote krachtreserve, souplesse,
zuinigheid en duurzaamheid, eigenen dit oer-soliede
type bizonder voor het groot-toerisme, hetzij met o
zonder zijspanwagen. Zoowel de man, die met zij
vrouw van zijn vrije middagen of Zondagen wil ge
nieten als de groot-tourist, die buitenlandsche tochte
wenscht te maken, vinden in deze in-betrouwbar
eenvoudig geconstrueerde Harley-Davidson alles w
zij zich maar kunnen voorstellen.

Reeds jaren geleden begon het motorrijwiel zijn
entree te doen bij de politie. Gaandeweg werd dit
gebruik grooter, met het gevolg, dat er thans hier
te lande bijna geen gemeente van beteekenis is,
of de politie bedient er zich van motorrijwielen.
Die goede gewoonte is gevolgd door de Mare-
chaussee, die ook sinds eenige jaren haar werk op motorrijwielen
verricht. Men weet bij die instanties, dat een motorrijwiel vóór
alles **eenvoudig, betrouwbaar** en **duurzaam** moet zijn. Het is dus
niet te verwonderen, dat in die diensten bijna uitsluitend Harley-
Davidson in gebruik is.

Contrôlelampjes voor smering en dynamo.
Balanceerend frictiepedaal 750
't Sterke, dubbele
op de zware


The 1938 two-cylinder models. The title page of this brochure from The Netherlands is shown on page 28.

**DE 80 – 1300 c.c. TWEE-CYLINDER**

De evenknie van de 1200 c.c., doch met meer inhoud,
dus nog grootere kracht. Men vraagt meer snelheid
met nog grootere krachtreserve: Harley-Davidson geeft
die zonder in een speciale sportmachine te vervallen.
Eenvoud en gemakkelijke behandeling blijven. De
betrouwbaarheid wint er mée. Dank zij de onderling
verwisselbare wielen, die ook de typen 1000 en
1200 hebben, een prachtcombinatie, niet alleen voor
politie- en ander dienstgebruik, maar ook voor den
groot-toerist, die iets van de wereld wil zien.

kleptuimelaars op 1000 c.c. model.
Onderling verbonden remschoenen.

Door de vele verbeteringen voor 1938
zullen Harley-Davidson-rijders opnieuw
grootere waarde voor hun geld verkrij-
gen. Van vele werkende deelen is de
levensduur verlengd. Het onderhoud is
gemakkelijker gemaakt. Grooter ge-
ruischloosheid is bereikt. Geen olieverlies;
grooter zindelijkheid. Verhoogd remver-
mogen — grootere veiligheid. Nog weer
verhoogd comfort. Grooter gemak in behandeling. En natuurlijk: onderhoudskos-
ten weder gereduceerd. Den gelukkigen
bezitter van een 1938 Harley-Davidson
wachten heerlijke dagen in het zadel!

**Het beste is altijd het goedkoopste**

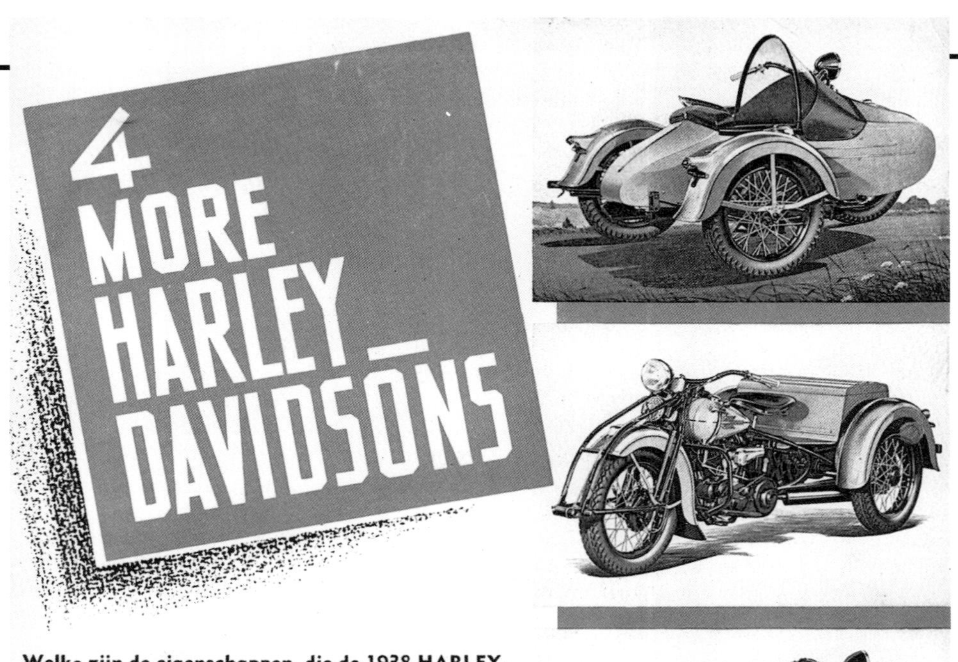

**Welke zijn de eigenschappen, die de 1938 HARLEY-DAVIDSONS onderscheiden van vorige typen?**

1. Roode en groene signaal-lampjes voor oliedruk en dynamo-lading.
2. Geslepen distributie-tandwielen op alle modellen.
3. Geheel ingesloten kleppenmechanisme op de 1000 c.c.
4. Onderling verbonden remschoenen op de zware modellen.
5. Extra-versterkte frames op de 1000, 1200 en 1300 c.c. modellen.
6. Zelf-centreerende vork-conus op de zware modellen.
7. Op de 750 c.c. zelfde schakel-mechanisme als op de zware modellen.
8. Distributie-tandwielen op de 750, 1200 en 1300 c.c. loopen thans in oliebad.
9. Bij alle modellen verbeterde olieleiding-nippels.
10. Verbeterd frictiepedaal bij de 750 c.c. (als in 1937 reeds op de zware modellen.)
11. Olie-afdichting klepbussen op 750, 1200 en 1300 c.c. verbeterd.
12. „Zerk"-alemite-nippels op alle modellen.
13. Fraaie kleurencombinatie met nieuwe bies.
14. **Sterk verlaagde prijzen.**

**Voor garages, winkelbedrijf etc. levert Harley-Davidson de beroemde, uiterst practische „Servicar". Beschrijving daarvan wordt op aanvrage gaarne toegezonden.**

# HARLEY-DAVIDSON M

## THE 61 OHV TWIN . . . .

The sensation of the motorcycle world, the 61 Overhead Valve Twin has gained the praise and admiration of riders everywhere who appreciate the latest in engineering advancements and who demand the utmost in a motorcycle. The performance of this great motorcycle out on the road and in competition, plus its ability to keep going over endless miles, is winning for it thousands upon thousands of new riders every season. For 1939, the 61 OHV is a still finer appearing motorcycle with a new, beautiful tail light, streamlined instrument panel, polished stainless steel fender strips, and attractive color scheme. A number of motor refinements make for still better performance, reduced operating costs, and longer motor life.

## THE 45 TWIN . . . . . .

A great favorite with solo riders, the 45 Twin is steadily gaining in popularity. In all kinds of competition events it has made an outstanding record. A straight-through lap on crankcase bearings, piston and ring changes, new valve springs, 24-needle roller bearings in the trans-

mission are 1939 advancements that will give owners the maximum in service and performance. A new ride control, with the side bars brought down below the handlebars, adds to safety and appearance. The 45 Twin and all other 1939 Harley-Davidsons are now fitted with self-aligning upper and lower head cones in the steering head. Easy handling is assured throughout the life of the motorcycle with no binding or pitting of ball bearings and races.

# TORCYCLES *for* 1939

## THE 74 TWIN . . . . . .

The acknowledged leader in side-valve motorcycles, the 74 Twin enjoys the distinction of having been chosen by more riders than any other make or model on the roads of America today. For solo, sidecar, Package Truck, pleasure, police, and commercial use, its enthusiastic owners are legion. Its powerful, quiet motor will deliver still more horsepower and still greater owner satisfaction and longer trouble-free service because of such 1939 advancements as steel-strutted pistons, oil-control piston rings, equalized cylinder lubrication, improved mani-

fold, perfected valve spring covers. In common with the 61OHV and 80 Twins, changes in clutch design have been incorporated that make for smoother clutch action, minimize clutch slippage, and assure easier shifting.

## THE 80 TWIN . . . . . .

Identical with the 74 Twin except for a still larger motor, the 80 Twin has made many friends because of its great reserve power. With the 61 and 74 Twins, it shares such 1939 features as a new clutch push rod thrust bearing in the transmission with 25 balls, each ¼" in diameter. On these three models, a sliding gear has been incorporated in the most used speeds for easier shifting. The sliding gear is in second gear position in the four speed transmission, and is in low gear position in the three speed, and in the three speed and reverse transmissions. All models have a new push-ball oil cup to provide adequate lubrication of the front brake cable. There is a new, neat stop light switch on all models, a new gasoline strainer, a drain-out plug at the bottom of the carburetor bowl, and saddle tops have a two-tone russet finish in rhino-grain.

STAMP
HERE
Come in—See—Ride . . .
the 1941 HARLEY-DAVIDSON
Centrifugally-controlled oil pump on all models • New design clutch on all models • Improved transmission on 45 Twins and Servi-Cars • New Big Twin muffler • Airplane-style speedometer face • Positive-grip hand brake lever • Giant air cleaner • Relocated police radio carrier • Better 45 Twin brakes • Many other improvements • New 74 OHV model • Beautiful color options • Lower prices on 61 OHV and 45 WLDR
PRINTED IN U.S.A.


The WLA 45, the military version of the famous 750 WLD, was born in 1941. The Model 74 OHV was new.

# Motocicletas HARLEY-DAVIDSON 1947

18.500,00

A VISTA DESCONTO 10%

a prazo { entrada 7.500,00 / 10 prest. 1.100,00

**_MODÊLO 750 c. c. Válvula Lateral_**

Êste modêlo é particularmente apreciado pelos motociclistas que não usam side-car.

É de fácil manejo, muito confortável e de consumo bastante econômico.

Seus cilindros duplos do tipo V e o seu motor de válvula lateral com um deslocamento do pistão de 45" desenvolvem surpreendente potência para vencer quaisquer caminhos e subidas.

A notável eficiência dêste modêlo é sempre uma fonte de inteira satisfação para o seu possuidor.

O assento com suporte de mola, uma particularidade da Harley-Davidson, o confortável selim bem acolchoado e forrado com finissimo couro, bem como os pneus balão proporcionam ao motociclista toda comodidade na viagem.

As rodas possuem aro central e são facilmente desmontáveis. Acabamento verde-oliva com filetes vermelhos e partes metáli-

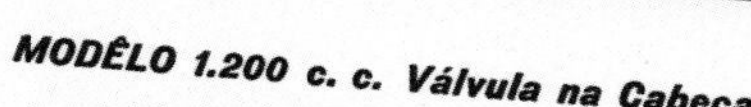

**_MODÊLO 1.200 c. c. Válvula na Cabeça_**

A incontestável eficiência do modêlo 61 despertou interêsse por um modêlo do mesmo tipo, mais potente e capaz de desenvolver maior velocidade.

O modêlo de 1.200 c. c. satisfaz a estas exigências do motociclista perito que insiste no que há de melhor como performance, tanto usando a motocicleta simples como com sidecar.

Novo mostrador de velocimetro, mais fácil de ler mesmo no escuro. Todas as motocicletas Harley-Davidson são equipadas com freios de expansão interna nas rodas dianteiras e trazeiras.

O freio trazeiro é acionado por pedal, e o dianteiro por alavanca, colocada no guidão.

Placa de mudança melhorada, cromada no lado do tanque, em todos os modêlos, facilitando os movimentos da motocicleta.

MOTOR HARLEY-DAVIDSON CYCLES

**_MODÊLO 1.200 c. c. Válvula Lateral_**

De todos os modêlos produzidos na America do Norte é êste o preferido pelos motociclistas de todo o mundo.

O seu funcionamento perfeito, à toda prova, faz dêle a moto favorita para qualquer uso: policia, comércio, recreio, sem ou com side-car.

Tem, como todos outros modêlos, uma válvula reguladora de gasolina, colocada no alto do tanque à esquerda, permitindo o uso imediato da gasolina de reserva.

Êstes modêlos são providos de estribos aerodinâmicos, dobráveis, colocados de modo a garantir o máximo conforto.

Os tanques dêstes modêlos são geminados e comunicam-se entre si.

As rodas dos side-cars são desmontáveis e intercambiáveis com às da motocicleta.

A brochure in Portuguese for Brazil. The 1200 was still available with either overhead or side valves.

Probably no Harley fan had expected a 125cc motor, but the little motorcycle — based on the popular German DKW RT 125 — went over splendidly and closed a gap in the market.

SPECIFICATIONS
MOTOR—Single unit motor and transmission. Air-cooled, two-cycle, single cylin-
der. Aluminum head. Linkert carburetor. Aluminum alloy, dome top piston.
Main bearings, ball type; connecting rod bearing, roller type. Drop-forged con-
necting rod. Bore, 2.0625". Stroke, 2.281". Compression ratio, 6.6.
TRANSMISSION—Harley-Davidson 3-speed. Constant mesh gears. Foot shift.
LUBRICATION—Lubricated by oil mixed with gasoline. Oil measuring cup is
attached to the underside of the gas cap.
IGNITION—Harley-Davidson waterproof, with a 6-pole shunt generator, voltage
regulator, 10 ampere-hour storage battery and coil.
ELECTRICAL EQUIPMENT — Adjustable, 5½", double filament headlight. Tail-
light. Disc-type horn operated from right handlebar. Stoplight kit available.
CLUTCH—Wet clutch, left handlebar operated. Torque capacity of 35 foot pounds.
FRAME—Single loop, reinforced tubular steel. Welded for great strength. Ball
bearing steering head bearings. Wheelbase, approximately 50".
FORKS—Rocker-type, pressed steel. Band-type rubber cushion and recoil springs.
MUFFLER—Specially designed for the Harley-Davidson single cylinder two-stroke.
TIRES—Goodyear or Firestone, 3.25 x 19". Oversize for maximum riding comfort.
BRAKES—Large, 5" internal expanding on each wheel. Front wheel brake
operated by lever on right handlebar. Rear wheel brake is right foot operated.
SPEEDOMETER — Built in headlight housing. Operated by cable from front hub.
TANKS—Saddle-type, welded steel. Capacity, 1½ U.S. gals.; reserve, ¼ U.S. gal.
The modern, economical, sporty way to get there and back!


The advertising slogans for the little Harley much resemble those that were used in Europe then.

GOOD PALS TOGETHER
FOR ERRANDS
NEWSPAPER DELIVERY
SHOPPING TRIPS
WEEK END JAUNTS
The fun-way to go places..at Low Cost!
HARLEY-DAVIDSON 125
LIGHT IN WEIGHT — EASY TO HANDLE
Safe, dependable power transportation that everyone can enjoy — everyone can afford
Here's fun for you . . . fun on wheels . . . the thrill of power taking you smoothly and comfortably wherever you want to go! Here are happier week ends and holidays, exciting outings, picnics, delightful sightseeing trips . . . all within easy reach at the twist of the throttle! And here's efficient, yet low-cost, transportation . . . for riding to school, to factory, store or office, for shopping, visiting, doing errands, making deliveries. Here, too, is freedom from buses and trolleys, from the need of always using your car! Here's power riding with a Harley-Davidson 125 . . . the fun way to go places . . . a modern, convenient travel method in tune with the times, suitable for any purpose, easy on any purse!
Economical! Owners say, "90 miles and more to the gallon!"
Owners of the 125 are amazed at the high mileage they get. Ninety miles to the gallon is average — some owners report even more. With only a gallon of gas, you say goodbye to filling stations for a long, long time.
Easy to ride! You learn in one lesson!
Anybody can ride the Harley-Davidson 125! It's so light, so well designed that it practically balances itself! Young or old can learn to handle it safely in just one trip around the block!
No parking problems!
The 125 takes so little room you can park it almost anywhere. It weighs so little you can move it easily. There is space for it in any garage.
It's the Slickest Thing on Wheels!
Printed in U.S.A.
BACK AND FORTH TO WORK
FOR PLEASURE
TO SCHOOL
TO SPORT EVENTS
OUTINGS AND PICNICS
VISITING FRIENDS
ON THE FARM

The advertising for the 125 was drawn with verve. The relatively economical little machine was intended mainly for younger buyers.

1948 was not only the year when a completely new Harley-Davidson was born. In this brochure for the 1949 model year, the drawing of the 125 is scarcely eye-catching alongside those of the bigger, more traditional machines . . .

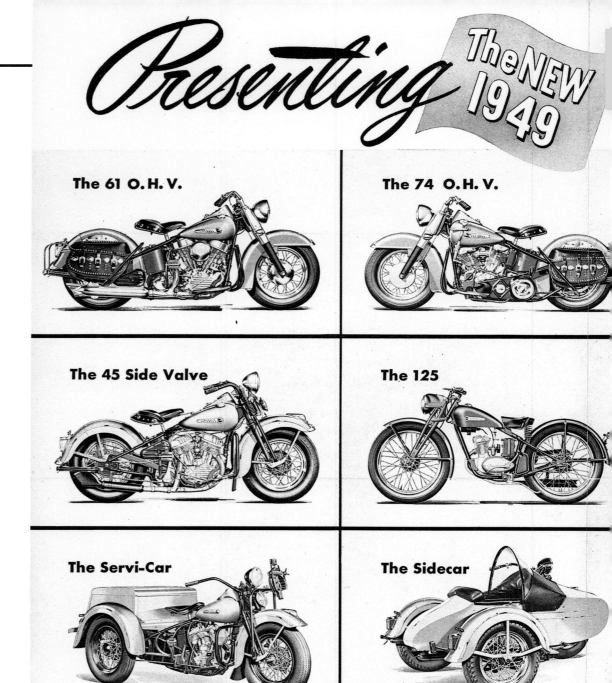

# Presenting The NEW 1949

The 61 O.H.V.

The 74 O.H.V.

The 45 Side Valve

The 125

The Servi-Car

The Sidecar

# arley-Davidsons

SUPERB riding comfort, greater handling ease, greater safety, streamlined design for outstanding beauty distinguish the Harley-Davidsons for 1949. A new era in motorcycle riding comfort is ushered in with the introduction of the Hydra-Glide fork on the 61 and 74 cubic inch O.H.V. models. Incorporating features found in no other fork of its type ever produced, it irons out bumps and washboard roads like magic. The impact is cushioned by long helical springs, supported and contained in the main tubes. The springs are hydraulically dampened by means of synthetic oil of high viscosity index. Hydraulic stops are provided in both recoil and cushion positions. Fork movement is now more than five inches, an increase of 100%. Rate of spring action is low for quick response to road inequalities. The road-hugging stability of the Hydra-Glide fork results in remarkable handling ease that is further enhanced by roller steering head bearings.

Greater night riding safety is achieved in the 61 and 74 cubic inch models with a new sealed ray headlight that makes 10-13% more light available to the rider. The double filament, 32-32 candle power, prefocused bulb, in conjunction with a larger, new-shaped reflector and lens, sends a path of light out from the motorcycle and eliminates the usual dead spot in the road ahead. In the lower beam, the light is intensified and dipped to the right. Oncoming drivers are not blinded, and the motorcycle rider plainly sees the edge of the road as well as pedestrians or other objects. The sealed ray unit is easily replaceable from any Harley-Davidson dealer's stock.

A new, more powerful front brake on the O.H.V. models, with 34% greater braking surface, is another safety factor for 1949. Brake acting lever is now located in the drum, where it is protected from the elements. Together with the efficient rear brake, the rider has positive braking power at his command.

Air flow fenders on the O.H.V. models add the last word in streamlining and beauty to these magnificent models. Formed under tremendous pressure, the front fender is in one piece and the rear fender is in two sections to accommodate the hinged feature. Glistening, stainless steel trim on front and rear fenders further enhances good looks. Chrome and stainless steel have been lavishly employed throughout the 1949 models.

To arrest rusting and discoloration, cylinders on all models, and the O.H.V. exhaust pipes are siliconed a beautiful silver. Mufflers on all models are siliconed in black. All models have grease-tight, water-tight, rubber handlebar grips of new design. Rubber mounted, chrome handlebars are obtainable for all Twins and provide additional comfort by isolating the rider from vibration and road shock. Numerous equipment groups are offered. Two new optional colors, in addition to black, Burgundy and Peacock Blue, and a third new color, Metallic Congo Green, is available at slight extra cost. For full information about the great line of Harley-Davidson motorcycles for 1949, see your dealer today.

**HARLEY-DAVIDSON MOTOR CO.**
**Milwaukee 1, Wisconsin, U.S.A.**

*Upper and lower roller bearings in fork head.*

*Prefocused, sealed ray headlight for greater night riding safety.*

*Exhaust pipes on O.H.V. models and all cylinders are siliconed.*

*34% more braking surface on the front brake on the O.H.V. models.*

★ *The Hydra-Glide fork responds to the slightest bump as well as to a deep chuck hole. With its more constant trail, this new fork gives the rider better control, easier handling, greater safety and sensational riding comfort.*

. . . and here's how the new 125 cycle looked.

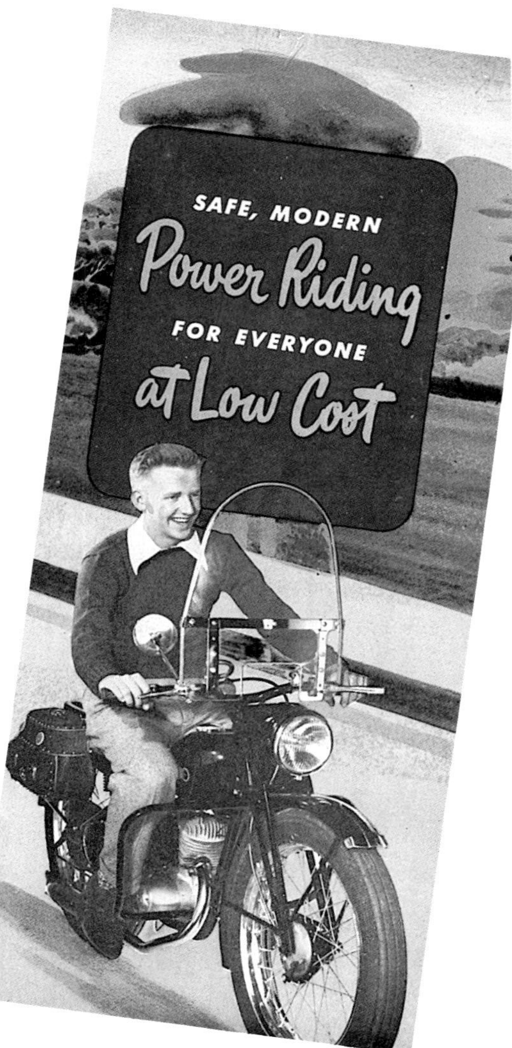

SAFE, MODERN
Power Riding
FOR EVERYONE
at Low Cost

Tuned to the times, made to meet modern motoring conditions, the Harley-Davidson 125 brings you new, personal transportation convenience . . . new experiences in fun and outdoor enjoyment! It's a two-wheeler everyone can ride, everyone can afford . . . young and old. Light in weight and perfectly balanced, the 125 handles so easily that you need no previous experience in order to learn to ride it safely.

You'll be agreeably surprised to discover how comfortably you zip over roads and streets on its big, balloon-tired wheels and cushioned springing . . . how smoothly and quietly its air-cooled motor purrs you on your way . . . how completely you can control every move with 3-way foot shift, easy-grip steering and handlebar throttle . . . how sure and safe it is with large, positive-action brakes on *both* wheels. Generator and battery provide powerful illumination for safe, night riding — regardless of the speed at which you travel.

There's a treat in store for you the first time you try a Harley-Davidson 125 . . . a pleasant surprise in practical, dependable, personal transportation . . . at amazingly low cost! Come in and take your FREE RIDE today!

## PRECISION CONSTRUCTION FOR REAL DEPENDABILITY

Sturdily built headlight features a handlebar operated, 21-21 candlepower bulb with dual beam control. Neatly curved headlight assembly also houses an accurate, cable-operated speedometer.

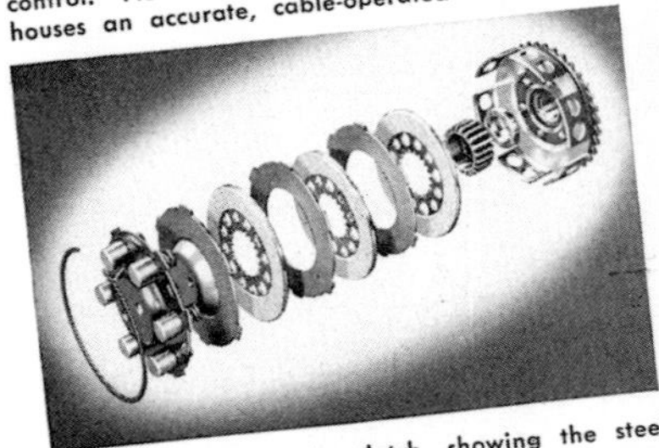

Exploded view of the clutch, showing the steel separator plates and friction discs. Clutch operates in an oil bath and is easily controlled by a lever conveniently mounted on the left handlebar.

Right side of the 125 features the ignition coil, voltage regulator, gear position indicator, rear brake foot pedal, right foot rest, horn, chrome exhaust pipe, specially designed, two-cycle muffler.

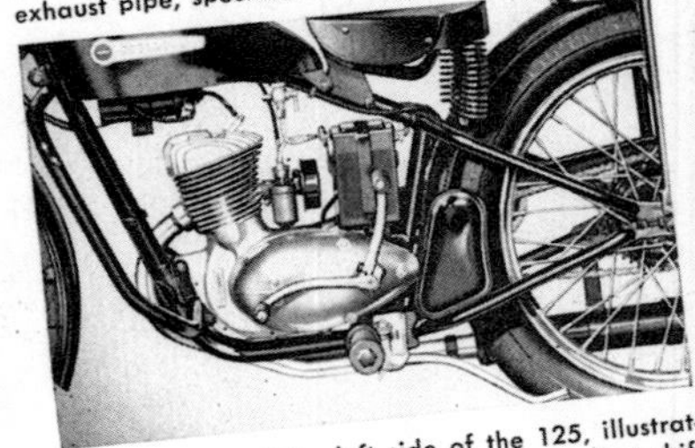

Close-up view of the left side of the 125, illustrating the sturdy, 10 ampere-hour battery, foot shift lever, kick starter, tool box, jiffy stand, left foot rest, carburetor, air cleaner and clutch case cover.

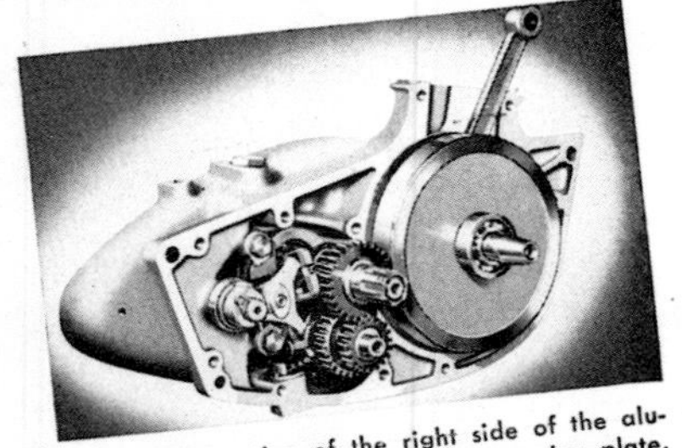

Cutaway illustration of the right side of the aluminum crankcase, showing the compression plate, main shaft ball bearing, constant mesh gears, and part of the shifting mechanism and connecting rod.

Right handlebar-operated, 5" front brake supplements right foot-operated rear wheel brake of equal size, providing maximum riding safety. Alemite-Zerk lubrication fitting on brake actuating arm.

Those in the know will soon recognize the source of the design.

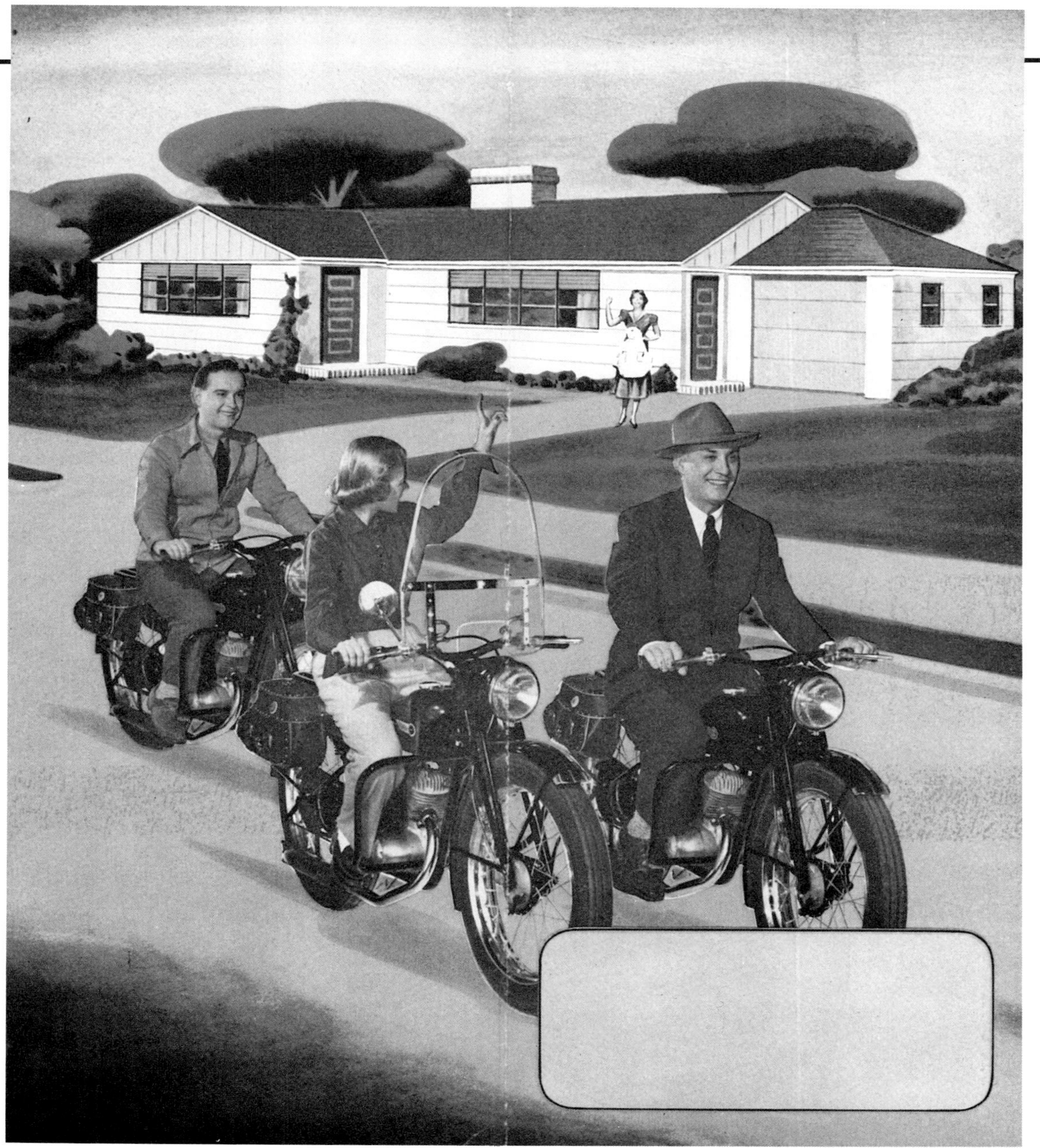

All of them are riding Harley-Davidsons except the "grass widow."

Now offered again in Germany: a 1949 Harley-Davidson brochure.

If you want to drive an extraordinary motorcycle — superior in performance, reliability and economy - here it is!
Model 750cc for the highest demands

Der außerordentlich bequeme Sattel, mit Schwammgummi-Polster und dauerhaftem Lederüberzug

**SATTEL:** HARLEY-DAVIDSON-Sattel mit der bekannten federnden Sattelstütze, dadurch einmalige Fahreigenschaften wie mit Hinterradfederung.

**VORDERGABEL:** HARLEY-DAVIDSON-Patent. Eine feste und eine federnde Gabel kombiniert.

**KRAFTSTOFFTANK:** Inhalt 12 Ltr. Benzin, 4 Ltr. Oel.

**LENKER:** HARLEY-DAVIDSON-Lenker mit Drehgriffen.

**GEWICHT:** 210 kg

**RADSTAND:** 1460 mm

**LÄNGE ÜBER ALLES:** 2120 mm

**FARBE:** Schwarz mit rotem Spiegel oder Silbergrau mit blauem Spiegel und mit einem Goldstreifen abgesetzt.

Dies sind einige der wichtigsten Merkmale, die seit mehr als vier Jahrzehnte HARLEY-DAVIDSON-Motorräder bekannt gemacht und sich bei schärfsten Prüfungen und im täglichen Gebrauch hervorragend bewährt haben.

IMPORTEUR:
FRIEDRICH VISÉ & Co. (Inh. Friedrich Visé) AACHEN, Brabantstr. 66/70
TELEFON 30504

Rudolf Kern, Druckerei, Nürnberg

..erst eine „HARLEY" fahren – und dann KAUFEN!

The extraordinarily comfortable saddle with foam rubber upholstery and a lasting leather cover.
SADDLE: HARLEY-DAVIDSON saddle with the well-known sprung seat post, giving unique riding characteristics as with rear suspension.
FRONT FORK: HARLEY-DAVIDSON patented, combining a fixed and a sprung fork.
FUEL TANK: Contains 12 liters of gasoline, 4 liters of oil.
HANDLEBARS: HARLEY-DAVIDSON handlebars with turning handles.
WEIGHT: 210 kilograms.
WHEELBASE: 1460 mm.
OVERALL LENGTH: 2120 mm.
COLORS: Black with red mirror or silver gray with blue mirror, and set off with a gold stripe.
These are some of the most important features that have made HARLEY-DAVIDSON motorcycles renowned for more than four decades, and that have proved themselves splendidly in the most stringent tests and in everyday use.
Importer: Friedrich Visé & Co. (Friedrich Visé prop.), Aachen, Brabantstrasse 66-70.

. . . first drive a "HARLEY" — and then buy it.

HARLEY-D

# 750 ccm Modell

Stabilität, Leistungsfähigkeit
räder. Schon vor 20 Jahren
Verbesserungen ihren grundsätzlichen Aufbau nicht zu verändern bra
lichkeit gewidmet. Hier haben Sie eine Maschine, die vor 20 Jahren
Im Laufe der Jahre mit allen Neuerungen der Technik ausgestattet, w
zu den wirtschaftlichsten überhaupt zählt.

Das stromlinienförmige Armaturengehäuse mit dem großen Tachometerkopf (bei Nacht beleuchtbar), den Signallampen, für Öldruck und Ladeanzeiger sowie Zünd- und Lichtschalter

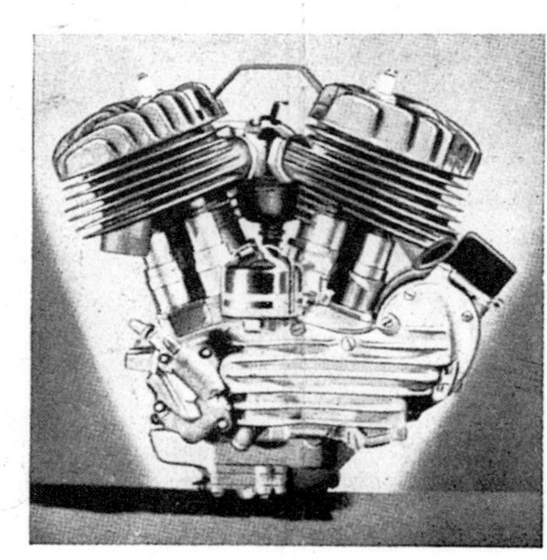

Motor des 750-ccm-Modells. Man beachte das Unterbrechergehäuse und die stark verrippten Leichtmetallzylinderköpfe

**MOTOR:** 2 Zylinder in V-Form, 4-Takt, Leichtmetall-Zylinderköpfe nach Ricardo-Patent. Kühlrippen in Stromform, auch bei stundenlangen hohen Geschwindigkeiten keine Überhitzung.

**ÖLUNG:** HARLEY-DAVIDSON-Umlaufschmierung, garantiert geringsten Verbrauch, ca. 1 Ltr. pro 1000 km.

**GETRIEBE:** HARLEY-DAVIDSON-3-Gang-Schubgetriebe. Einfachste und unverwüstliche Ausführung. Für Beiwagenbetrieb kann Rückwärtsgang eingebaut werden.

**KUPPLUNG:** Mehrscheibenkupplung mit Fußbedienung.

HARLEY-D

750cc Model

Stability, performance and beauty have characterized HARLEY-DAVIDSON motorcycles for decades. This machine had attained such a perfection of form twenty years ago that all its technical improvements have not needed to change its basic design. The greatest emphasis have been placed on safety, comfort and economy. Here you have a machine that was first put on the market 20 years ago and made its way to almost every country in the world. During the course of the years, having been equipped with all the technical innovations, this model has become a motorcycle that ranks among the most economical in use and maintenance.

A V I D S O N

chönheit kennzeichnen seit Jahrzehnten die HARLEY-DAVIDSON-Motor-
diese Maschine so vollendet ihre Form gefunden, daß alle technischen
. Größten Wert wurde hier der Sicherheit, Bequemlichkeit und Wirtschaft-
lig auf den Markt gebracht, den Weg in fast alle Länder der Erde fand.
ieses Modell zu einem Motorrad, welches in Verbrauch und Unterhaltung

Durch die hochwirksamen Innenbackenbremsen an Vorder- und Hinterrad hat der Fahrer die Maschine vollkommen in seiner Gewalt

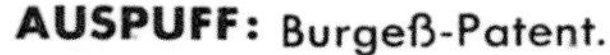

**AUSPUFF:** Burgeß-Patent.

**RÄDER:** Schnell auszubauen (Steckachse).

**BREMSEN:** Große und breite Vorder- und Hinterrad-Innenbacken-Bremsen.

**VERGASER:** Schebler-Patent, Kraftstoffverbrauch ca. 4 Ltr. pro 100 km bei mittlerer Geschwindigkeit.

**ANTRIEB:** Getriebekette Duplex, in Ölbad, links. Hinterradkette rechts offen, einfach abgedeckt. Beide Ketten werden von der automatischen Pumpe geschmiert.

**RAHMEN:** Rohrrahmen mit im Gesenk geschmiedeten Steuerkopf und Verbindungen.

So einfach ist das Hinterrad herauszunehmen

A V I D S O N

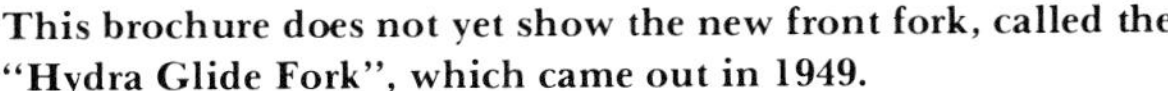

This brochure does not yet show the new front fork, called the "Hydra Glide Fork", which came out in 1949.

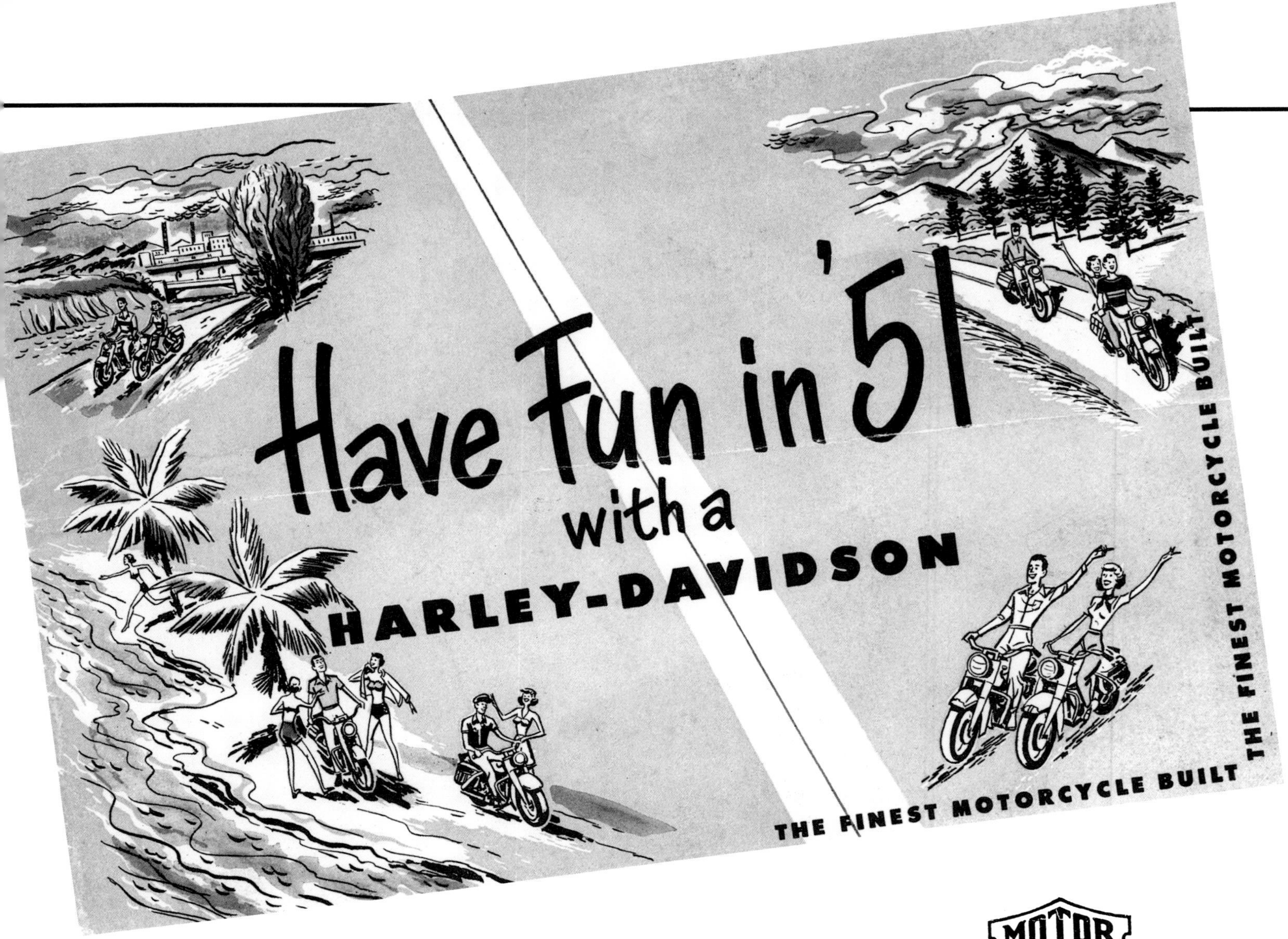

Have Fun in '51
with a
HARLEY-DAVIDSON

THE FINEST MOTORCYCLE BUILT

THE FINEST MOTORCYCLE BUILT

Title page of a very interesting 1951 Harley-Davidson catalog. It consists of 16 pages and describes the 61 OHV, 74 OHV, 45 SV and 125 models.

This is "the" classic Harley — with 1200cc motor, big fenders and the leather saddlebags in cowboy-saddle style.

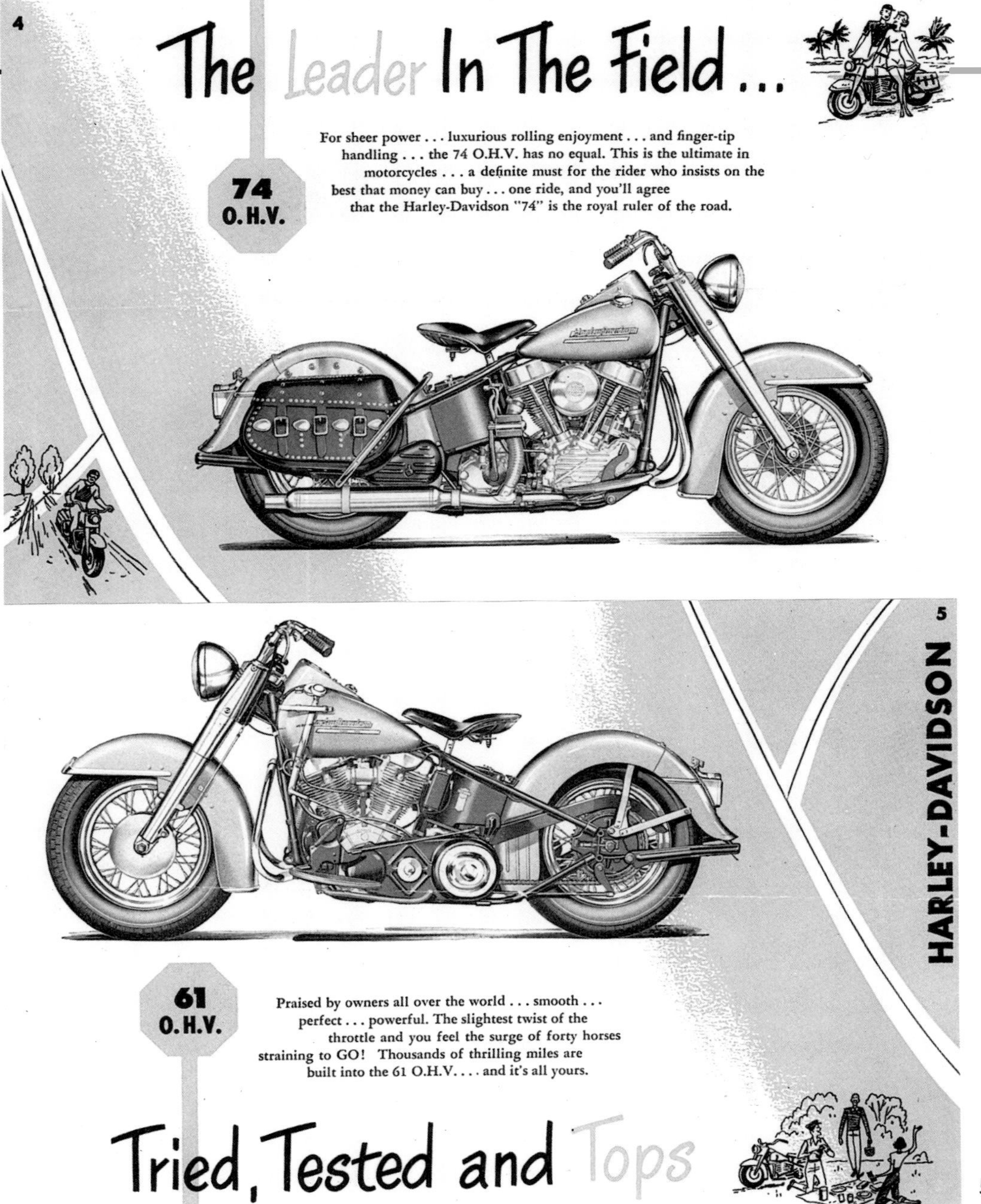

4
The Leader In The Field...
74 O.H.V.
For sheer power . . . luxurious rolling enjoyment . . . and finger-tip handling . . . the 74 O.H.V. has no equal. This is the ultimate in motorcycles . . . a definite must for the rider who insists on the best that money can buy . . . one ride, and you'll agree that the Harley-Davidson "74" is the royal ruler of the road.
5
HARLEY-DAVIDSON
61 O.H.V.
Praised by owners all over the world . . . smooth . . . perfect . . . powerful. The slightest twist of the throttle and you feel the surge of forty horses straining to GO! Thousands of thrilling miles are built into the 61 O.H.V. . . . and it's all yours.
Tried, Tested and Tops

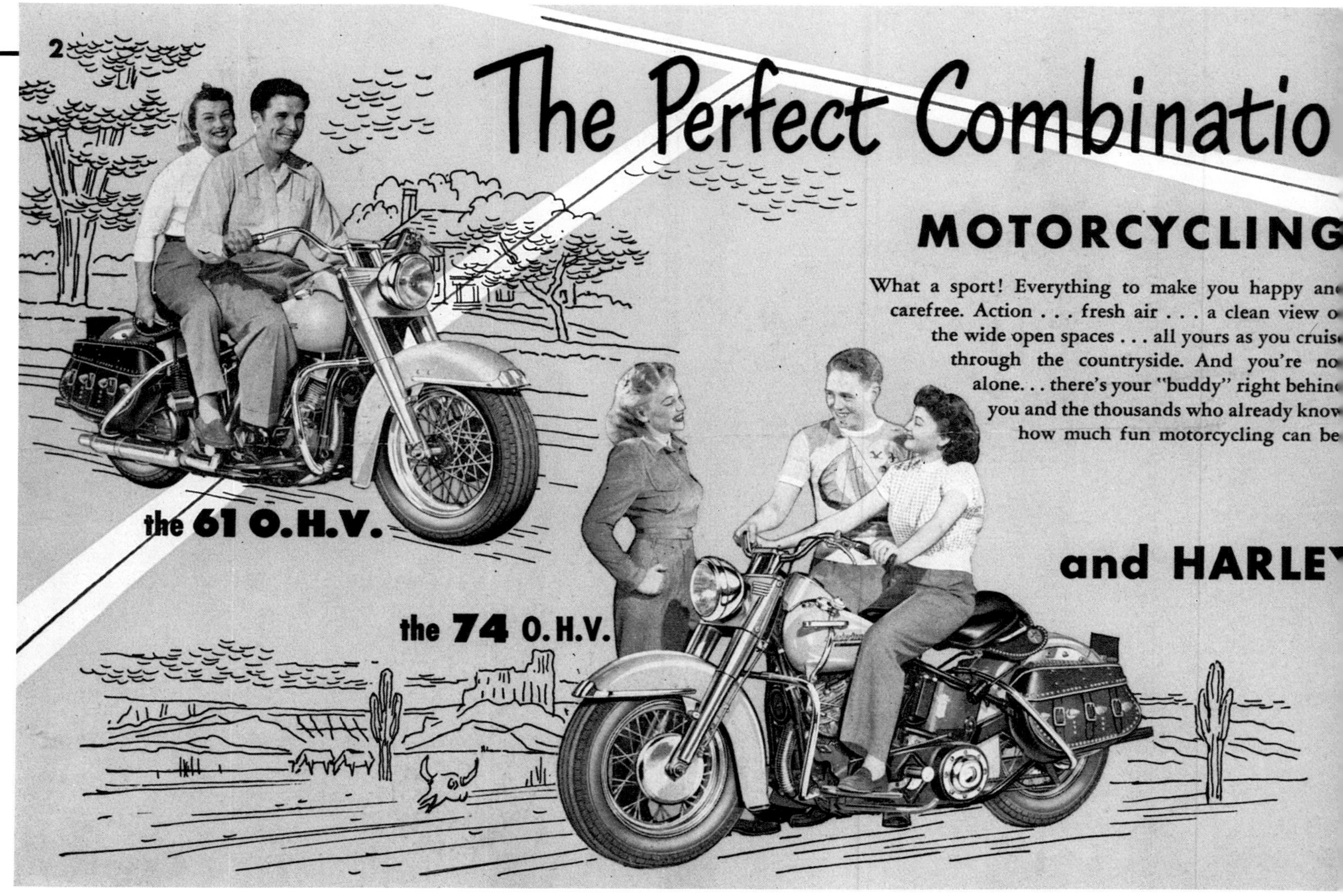
2
The Perfect Combinatio
MOTORCYCLING
What a sport! Everything to make you happy an
carefree. Action . . . fresh air . . . a clean view o
the wide open spaces . . . all yours as you cruis
through the countryside. And you're no
alone. . . there's your "buddy" right behin
you and the thousands who already know
how much fun motorcycling can be
the 61 O.H.V.
and HARLE
the 74 O.H.V.

3
or Wonderful Times
the
125
SIDECAR
AVIDSON MOTORCYCLES
the
45 Side Valve
Get the most out of the finest outdoor sport in the world . . . ride a Harley-Davidson and leave your troubles behind. Here is a motorcycle with the snap and styling you'll be proud to show off on every occasion. Safe . . . strong . . . streamlined . . . ready to take you anywhere, any time you please. It has no equal.

Here are all the 1951 Harley models at one glance. Even the little 125 (upper right) looks like a big machine here — but has all its attributes!

45
Side Valve
Harley-Davidson
Dollar-for-dollar, you can't match the big value of the Harley-Davidson 45 Side Valve. Economy . . . long life . . . beauty . . . rugged power . . . an outstanding favorite of the motorcycling world with a large gallery of boosters.
America's Greatest Motorcycle Value . . .

The 750 (45 SV) also ranks among the classics by now.

the
SIDECAR
Friend or family, whoever your companion . . . the Harley-Davidson Sidecar doubles your enjoyment of a wonderful sport all year around. Sleek lines . . . sturdy design . . . and smart finishes to match your Harley-Davidson.
HARLEY-DAVIDSON

Still popular: the sidecar.

11
BIG TWIN FEATURES

New safety bar designed for increased rider protection. Stronger, better looking. All tubular construction more flexible.


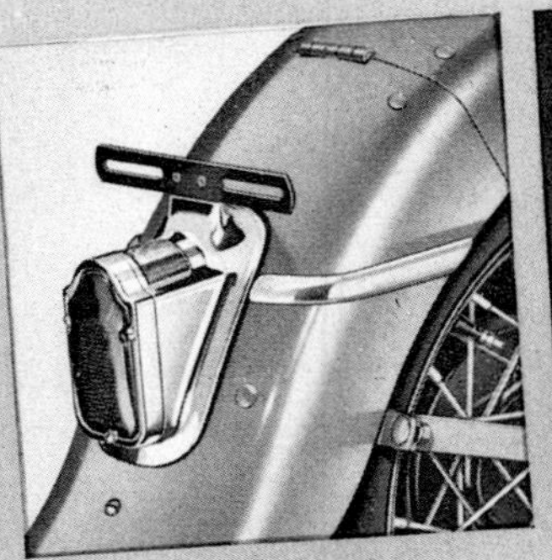

Streamlined fender trim of stainless steel. In harmony with new nameplate and front fender trim.


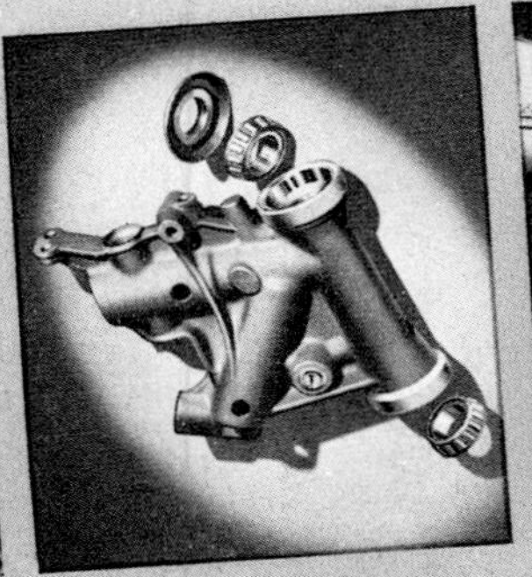

Steering head houses self-aligning, roller bearings and handy, theft-proof lock.


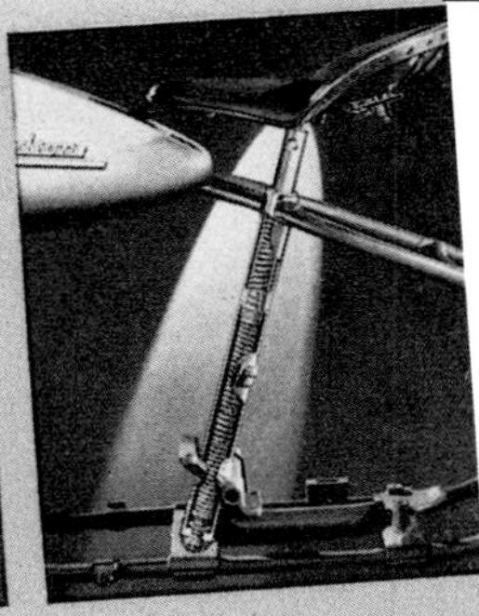

Saddle mounts on an adjustable seat post for jar-free riding. Also on the 45 Twin.

Famous Hydra-Glide fork "irons out" bumps and ruts, making for floating, smooth-riding comfort.

Internal expanding front and rear brakes for safe riding. Fully enclosed, waterproof, front brake left handlebar-operated, rear brake right foot-operated. Durable linings.

Tubular, streamlined, mellow-toned muffler with heavy gauge steel inner tube and end bells. Sound is deeper and more pleasing.
It's HARLEY-DAVIDSON for comfort, dependability and long service


Details of the 1951 Harley-Davidson Twins.

## the 74 and 61 O.H.V.

**MOTOR**—74 cu. in., air-cooled, four-stroke, V-type twin cylinder. Overhead valves in removable, aluminum cylinder heads. Hydraulic valve lifters assure constant tappet adjustment. Cam-ground, aluminum alloy piston with chrome plated compression rings. 1¼" crank pin and 3/16" rollers. All main bearings of retained roller type. Bore, 3-7/16". Stroke, 3-31/32". Horsepower, 53-55.

**MOTOR**—61 cu. in., air-cooled, four-stroke, V-type twin cylinder. Overhead valves in removable, aluminum cylinder heads. Hydraulic valve lifters assure constant tappet adjustment. Cam-ground, aluminum alloy piston with chrome plated compression rings. 1¼" crank pin and 3/16" rollers. All main bearings of retained roller type. Bore, 3-5/16". Stroke, 3½". Horsepower, 39-42.

**CARBURETOR**—Linkert, easily adjusted. Venturi opening 1⅛" on "61" and 1-5/16" on "74".

**TRANSMISSION**—Four speed with constant-mesh gears. Three speed and reverse with sliding low gear available at small extra cost.

**IGNITION**—Generator, storage battery, spark coil, circuit breaker. Waterproof. No troublesome distributor.

**ELECTRIC EQUIPMENT**—New, sealed ray headlight with prefocused 32-32 candlepower, double-filament bulb. Dual beam control. High output generator with automatic increase when lights are on. Storage battery. Disc-type horn.

**CLUTCH**—Super-service, multiple dry disc, left foot-operated.

**DRIVE**—Motor to transmission by automatically lubricated double-row roller chain. ⅝" pitch roller chain to rear wheel.

**FRAME**—Extra low, reinforced, double loop, trussed frame made from seamless steel tubing with major fittings drop-forged. Parkerized to resist rust. Wheel base 60½". Theft-proof lock.

**FRONT FORKS**—Hydra-Glide fork irons out bumps and washboard roads. Load is transmitted by long helical, oil-cushioned springs supported and contained in main tubes. Timken roller bearing steering head bearings.

**BRAKES**—Front and rear wheel, fully enclosed, waterproof.

**TIRES**—Goodyear or Firestone, 4-ply, 5.00" x 16" tires available in equipment groups.

**SADDLE**—Comfortable, form-fitting, mounted on cushion spring, seat post. Foam-rubber padded. Sport solo deluxe saddle with Royalite top at small extra cost.

**FINISH**—Over rust and corrosion resistant surfaces. Available in Persian Red, Brilliant Black, and Rio Blue. Available at extra cost: Metallic Green, Metallic Blue, and White. Silver for police service only. Frame is finished in black enamel.

## the 125 Model

**MOTOR**—Single unit motor and transmission. Air-cooled, two cycle, single cylinder. Aluminum head. Linkert carburetor. Aluminum alloy, dome-top piston without deflector. Full-floating, lock-ring retained, 9/16" piston pin. Drop-forged connecting rod with needle bearings on upper end. Main bearings of the ball type. Roller-type connecting rod bearings. Bore, 2.0625". Stroke, 2.281". Compression ratio, 6.6 to 1.

**TRANSMISSION**—Harley-Davidson three speed. Constant-mesh gears. Foot shift.

**LUBRICATION**—Engine is lubricated by oil mixed with the gasoline.

**IGNITION**—Harley-Davidson waterproof, with a 6-pole, 4-brush, shunt generator, voltage regulator, 10 ampere hour storage battery and coil.

**ELECTRICAL EQUIPMENT**—New, large, 7" prefocused, double filament headlight, dual-beam control from handlebar. Streamlined tail light. Disc-type horn operated from right handlebar.

**CLUTCH**—Operates in oil bath, left handlebar lever operated, multiple disc type. Torque capacity, 35 foot-pounds.

**FRAME**—Single loop, reinforced tubular steel, sturdy construction. Drop-forged steering head, ball bearing steering head bearings. Wheel base, approximately 50".

**FENDERS**—New, large, better looking more protective fenders. Five inches wide and flared at ends. Makes for over-all streamlined appearance.

**FORKS**—New, Tele-Glide telescopic spring fork for easy, road-cushioning riding. Sturdy springs absorb road shocks and makes for neat appearing, compact front end construction. Alemite-Zerk fittings on fork bearings.

**MUFFLER**—New, longer, more effective. Less restriction results in a definite increase in power. End design changed from fish-tail to tubular type.

**BRAKES**—Large, 5" internal expanding brake on each wheel. Front wheel brake is operated by lever on the right handlebar. Rear wheel brake is right foot operated.

**SADDLE**—American style, 1½" foam-rubber filled, comfortable, form fitting, bucket type saddle. Top of fine, pliable, weatherproof leather.

**FINISH**—Over rust and corrosion resistant surfaces. Standard colors: Rio Blue, Persian Red, Sportsman's Yellow. Available at small extra cost: Metallic Green, and Metallic Blue.

## the SIDECAR

**FRAME**—Seamless steel tubing, strongly reinforced and heat-treated at all points of stress. Aluminum passenger step plate attached to frame.

**WHEEL**—Quickly detachable wire wheel interchangeable with wheels on motorcycle. Roller bearing hub. Alemite lubricated.

**TIRE**—Goodyear or Firestone; 5.00" x 16" in equipment groups.

**BRAKE**—Internal expanding, waterproof, operated with rear wheel brake on motorcycle, providing three-wheel braking.

**SPRINGS**—Two easy-riding, special semi-elliptic with friction strap snubbers.

**TREAD**—49 inches.

**LUBRICATION**—Springs and shackles fitted with oil impregnated bushings, require no manual lubrication.

**BODY**—Beautifully streamlined. Built of heavy gauge, cold rolled auto body steel. Floor covered with composition matting. Luggage compartment. Padded arm rests.

**FINISH**—Available in Persian Red, Brilliant Black, and Rio Blue. Available at extra cost: Metallic Green, and Metallic Blue, and White. Silver for police service only. All black running gear.

## the 45 Side Valve

**MOTOR**—45 cu. in. side valve motor. Air-cooled, four-stroke, V-type. Cylinders, Silicone coated. Removable cylinder heads. Linkert carburetor. Motor develops 23 to 25 horsepower. Bore, 2¾". Stroke, 3-13/16".

**TRANSMISSION**—Harley-Davidson three speed. Full sliding dog clutches. Constant-mesh design.

**IGNITION**—Generator, storage battery, spark coil, circuit breaker. No distributor. Waterproof.

**ELECTRIC EQUIPMENT**—Large 7" headlight with prefocused double-filament bulb. Dual beam control. Built-in tail light. Stop light. High output generator with automatic increase when lights are on. 22-ampere hour storage battery. Disc-type horn.

**CLUTCH**—Harley-Davidson multiple dry disc; left foot-operated.

**DRIVE**—Motor to transmission by automatically lubricated, double-row roller chain; ⅝" pitch single-row roller chain to rear wheel.

**FRAME**—Reinforced tubular steel. Drop-forged and heat-treated head, motor and transmission brackets. Wheel base, 57½".

**FRONT FORKS**—Main and spring forks of seamless carbon steel tubing. Entire assembly heat-treated. Self-aligning steering head bearings.

**TIRES**—Goodyear or Firestone. 5.00" x 16" tires available in equipment groups.

**BRAKES**—Front and rear wheel, fully enclosed, waterproof.

**SADDLE**—Large, form-fitting, mounted on adjustable, cushion-spring seat post. Foam-rubber padded, covered with genuine leather. Sport solo deluxe saddle with Royalite top at small extra cost.

**FINISH**—Over rust and corrosion resistant surfaces. Available in Persian Red, Rio Blue, and Brilliant Black. Available at extra cost: Metallic Blue, Metallic Green, and White.

14

# HARLEY-DAVIDSON builds the finest motorcycle you can buy

HOW

The finished product is truly something beautiful to see . . . but have you ever stopped to think how much thought, skill and work goes into producing a Harley-Davidson motorcycle? It takes the highest caliber technical knowledge and craftsmanship . . . it takes the finest materials available . . . and it takes the complete cooperation of scores of shop men, designers, clerks and executive help. That's why Harley-Davidson motorcycles are the finest in the field . . . that's why you can be sure of a full measure of pleasure from your efficient and dependable Harley-Davidson. On this page are just a few of the many scientific methods used in producing the world's best motorcycle. These processes demand the most advanced equipment, facilities and machinery that represent an investment of millions of dollars, all to insure the high quality of your Harley-Davidson.

Left—ELECTRONICS
Handlebar grips of the Model 125 are made strong and long-lasting by the magic of electronic silver brazing of attachments.

Right—GAS BRAZING
Gas chemistry technique used in scale-free brazing of Model 125 steering head to frame. Makes for more durable connection.

Left—BONDERIZING
Gas-fired drying oven removes moisture from 5-stage bonderizing system. Bonderizing protects metal surface with phosphate coat.

Right—HONING
Cylinders are honed to within 1/1000 inch of engineer's specifications to give you smoother operation and long motor life.

The Harley-Davidson firm was the only surviving motorcycle manufacturer in America and took pride in its decades of experience.

The array of Harley-Davidson accessories was always extensive. And chrome decoration had played a particular role for years.

13
Foam-rubber-filled Buddy Seat designed for long hours on the road. Attractive trim. Covered with top-grade leather. Foot rests.
Attractive, all-plastic windshield for Hydra-Glide model. Will not crack or discolor.
Gracefully curved chrome rear bumper of durable construction. Protects fender and rear light.
WISCONSIN
1950
Chrome-plated spotlights for Hydra-Glide model. Easily mounted on fork. Hi-quality pre-focused bulb. Fog lenses are available.
ACCESSORIES
to give you more motorcycling enjoyment....
Here are just a few of the many accessory values provided by Harley-Davidson to add to your motorcycling fun. Enhance the beauty of your motorcycle . . . dress comfortably and attractively . . . form a club . . . or give your "buddy" a gift. Your Harley-Davidson dealer will be glad to show you this complete line of fine accessories . . . go in and see him soon.
Attractive, chrome-plated front bumper. Large, well-made. Mudguard protection.
Large, "carry-all" saddle bags. Bright nickel trim and spots. Made of high quality cowhide.
Chrome-plated oil filter keeps oil at top lubricating efficiency. Filters out harmful grit and dust. Adds to engine performance.

Two-tone 1956 brochure. Four years earlier, the K Model had replaced the old WL. In 1954 the K became a KH (55 cubic inches). They were especially happy to use racing success in advertising.

# Choice of the Champions

Champions across the Nation go for the winning ways of the Model K's. Watch the winners cross the finish line and you'll see the "K's" get the checkered flag time after time.

On track and road courses . . . cross country . . . on hard surfaces and on the sandy speedways . . . the "K's" get out in front and stay there to the finish.

Champions ride the winner . . . and the "K's" are winning more national championships than all other brands combined!

Joe Leonard

Everett Brashear

Billy Meier

Brad Andres

Paul Goldsmith

## NATIONAL CHAMPIONS AND NATIONAL CHAMPIONSHIPS

### 1954

| Championship | Event |
|---|---|
| 10-Mile National Championship | ½-Mile Dirt Track |
| 100-Mile National Championship | Road Race |
| 75-Mile National Championship | Road Race |
| 20-Mile National Championship | Mile Dirt Track |
| 50-Mile National Championship | Road Race |
| 8-Mile National Championship | ½-Mile Dirt Track |
| 25-Mile National Championship | Mile Dirt Track |
| National Championship | T.T. Races—45 cu. in. |
| National Championship | T.T. Races—80 cu. in. |
| 7-Mile National Championship | ½-Mile Dirt Track |
| 100-Mile National Championship | Mile Dirt Track |
| 8-Mile National Championship | Mile Dirt Track |
| 9-Mile National Championship | ½-Mile Dirt Track |

### 1955

| Championship | Event |
|---|---|
| 200-Mile National Championship | Beach-Road Race |
| 5-Mile National Championship | ½-Mile Dirt Track |
| 10-Mile National Championship | ½-Mile Dirt Track |
| 100-Mile National Championship | Road Race |
| 75-Mile National Championship | Road Race |
| 50-Mile National Championship | Road Race |
| 20-Mile National Championship | Mile Dirt Track |
| 8-Mile National Championship | ½-Mile Dirt Track |

The sporting K Model and its 1954 and 1955 victories. In the 900cc class this machine was naturally always the leader for want of competition.

SCRAMBLING . . . TOUR
CRUISING
NO MATTER HOW YOU RIDE . . .
Ride number 1 in the
on the road . . . on the trails
. . . anywhere
The "K's" are rapidly becoming the most popular motorcycle in America . . . riders everywhere are raving about the "do-all" versatility of this exciting series of Harley-Davidsons.
Ride it on the highway . . . on winding country roads . . . cross country . . . on the trails. Ride it anywhere . . . any way . . . and you'll find it the finest you've ever ridden.
Here's flashing speed . . . terrific dig-out . . . smooth handling . . . and the kind of riding comfort only hydraulic shocks can give you.
The new "K's" are on display at your Harley-Davidson dealer, right now.
See . . . and ride the No. 1 motorcycle in the Nation
KHK
Riding
. . . one
that's d
. . . that
will move
keep you
If you wa
motorcycle
Ride the K
KHK custom
peak performa
Polished head and
winning ways.
Heavier kick starter crank gear plate makes for more positive disengagement of kick starter mechanism.
Smooth operating, seven-plate clutch is built to take it for many thousands of carefree miles.
HARLEY-DAVIDSON MOTOR CO.
Milwaukee 1, Wis. U.S.A.
Increased gear strength and increased number of gear dogs make for even stronger, more durable transmission.

In shirt sleeves, without a helmet . . . safety regulations, otherwise an American domain, were still quite lax at that time!

Below: The technical data of the K models of 1956. 55 cubic inches provided 900cc displacement, but no performance statistics are stated.

R PLUS . . . THE EXCITING KHK!
K is like riding a rocket to the moon
rottle and . . . ZOOM! Here's a model
e rider who wants that extra power
ere's breathtaking acceleration that
ont of the pack in a hurry . . . and
ter mile.
better than the best . . . this is the
he thrilling difference.
KHK
New, lower frame and lower saddle position for easier handling and greater riding comfort.

HARLEY-DAVIDSON

KH · KHK

SPECIFICATIONS

**engine—kh model**—55 cu. in. air-cooled, four stroke, V-type twin cylinder side valve engine. Removable aluminum alloy cylinder heads. Enclosed valve gear. Low expansion aluminum alloy, cam-ground pistons. Cylinder bores honed and parkerized. Deep cylinder fins extend around intake and exhaust ports for proper cooling. All main bearings retained roller type; double tapered Timken bearings on the sprocket side; straight retained roller bearing on the gear side. Linkert carburetor. The size of the bore is 2¾". The length of the stroke is 4⁹⁄₁₆.

**khk model**—Above specifications plus high-lift cams; streamlined, mirror-polished intake and exhaust ports; polished combustion chamber in cylinder heads; needle-bearing roller tappets.

**transmission**—Harley-Davidson four speed. Incorporated as an integral part of crankcase casting. Sliding dog clutches. Large, rugged gears for durability. Constant-mesh design. Foot shift, hand clutch.

**lubrication**—Circulating lubrication system with gear-type pressure pump and gear-type scavenger pump with pressure feed direct to cylinder walls. Transmission and front chain lubricated by oil supply separate from engine. All other bearings Alemite-Zerk fitted.

**ignition**—Two-brush shunt, voltage controlled generator, storage battery, spark coil, circuit breaker. Easy starting and waterproof.

**clutch**—Harley-Davidson multiple dry disc. Left hand operated.

**drive**—Motor to transmission by ⅜" pitch triple chain running in oil bath and adjusted by sliding shoe. ⅝" pitch single-row roller chain to rear wheel.

**rear suspension**—Swing-arm type sprung by means of two helical coil springs and controlled by means of two hydraulic, automotive type shock absorbers, all enclosed in chrome covers. Pivot point of swinging arm is supported by pre-loaded Timken bearings.

**front fork**—Easy riding hydraulic fork. Load is transmitted by long helical springs supported and contained in main tubes, hydraulically dampened by oil of high viscosity index. Hydraulic stops are provided in both recoil and cushion positions.

**tires**—Goodyear or Firestone, 3.50 x 18.

**brakes**—Fully enclosed, front and rear brakes with molded anti-score lining. Front and rear brakes 8" in diameter and 1" wide.

**tanks**—Extra large welded heavy gauge steel gas tank with center filling cap. Capacity: 4½ gals., with reserve in addition. Reserve controlled by two-way gas valve with fuel strainer. Welded heavy gauge steel oil tank. Capacity: 3 quarts, with provision for filter. Oil tank has secure, screw-down provision.

**special equipment**—This model available with the Deluxe Group.

**finish**—Harmonizing two-tone color styling: Pepper Red with White tank panel; Atomic Blue with Champion Yellow tank panel; Champion Yellow with Black tank panel and Black with Champion Yellow tank panel. See your Harley-Davidson dealer for other available colors and color combinations. Chrome and stainless steel trim.

*Ask your Harley-Davidson dealer about his liberal trade-in allowances and easy-pay plans*

**Harley-Davidson-Import**
seit 1924

**GEORG SUCK**
**Hamburg-St.**
**Hagenbeckstr. 1-5 - Ruf 40 85 65**

## Choice of riders everywhere

Victory after victory in every type of racing event, has proved the dependability, stamina, roadability and handling ease of the Model K's. These are the very advantages and superiorities that every rider wants in his *own* motorcycle—and that's why more and more riders are making their "motor" a sparkling new "K"—how about *you?*

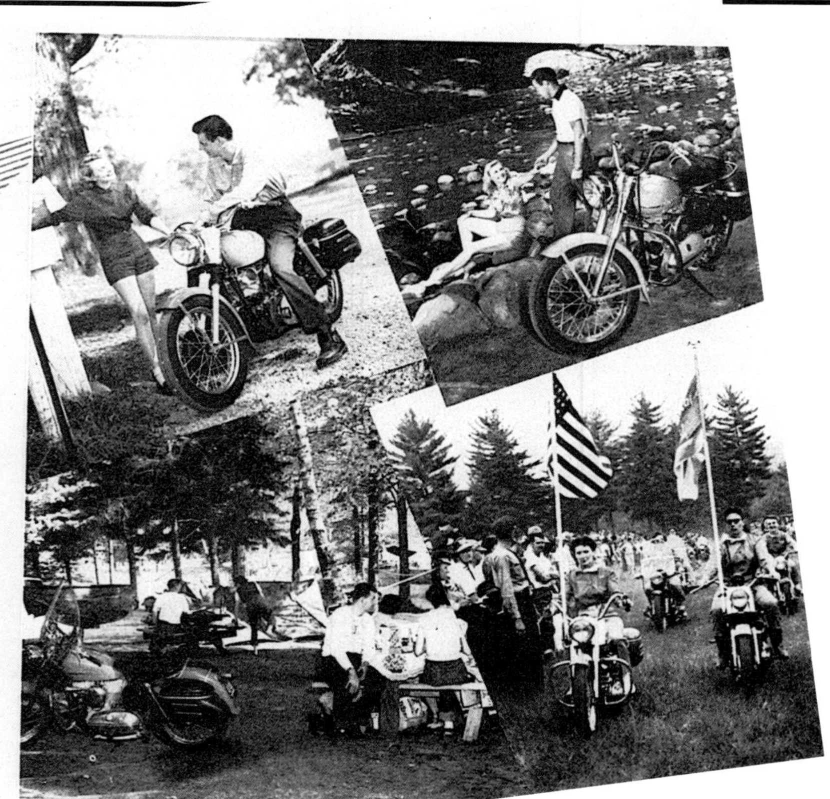

**Motorcycle traveling and club meetings were the parameters of sporting activity. The "alternative" motorcycle scene was not yet mentioned, the world was pure and without Hell's Angels.**

Happy Days — the motto of the mid-Fifties. Korea was over, and the economy was growing everywhere. And the one-cylinder 125 was still popular.

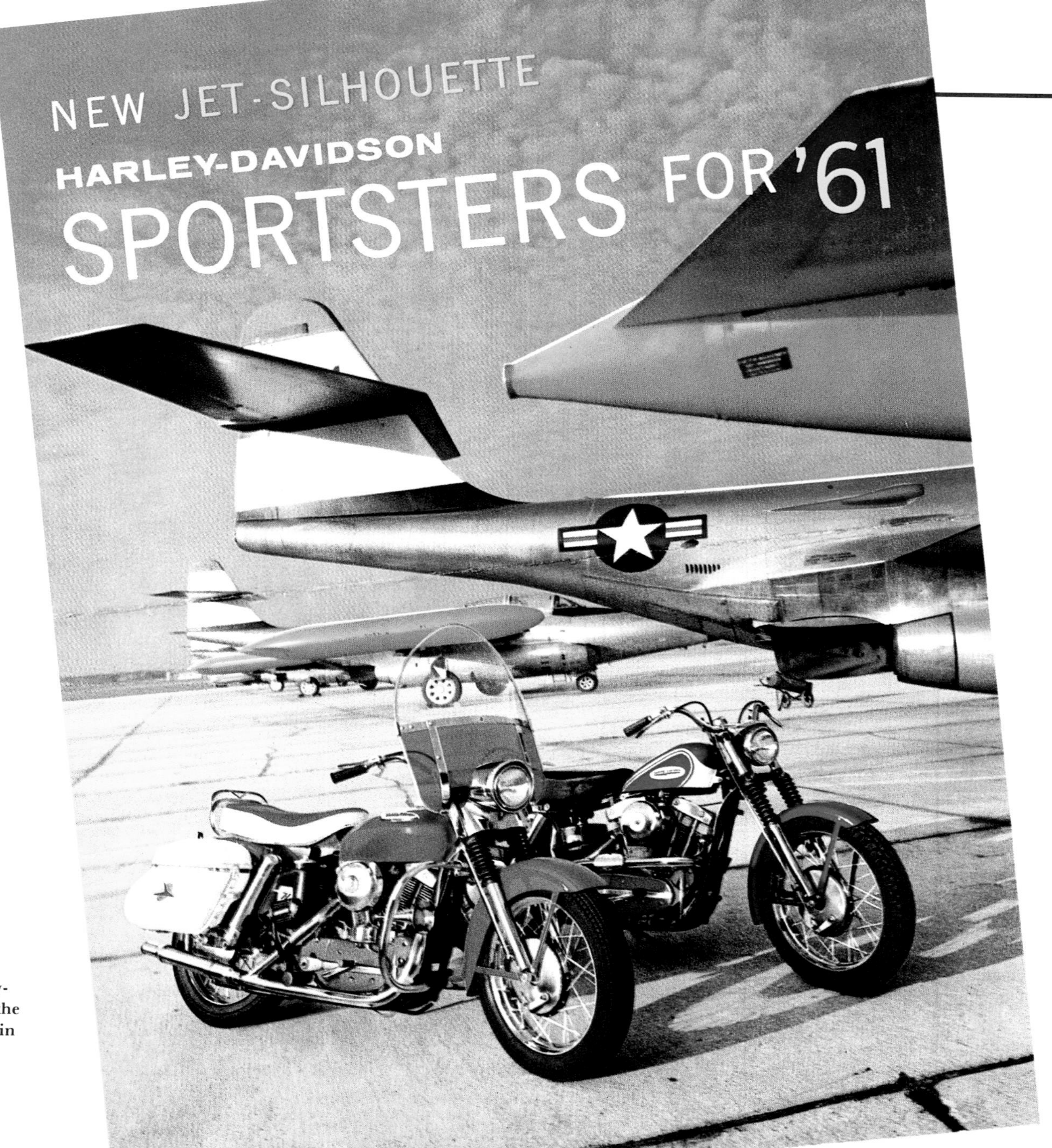


In 1960-61 Harley-Davidson scored the best sales records in its history.

Hottest Thing Going On two Wheels
SPORTSTER
H
electrifying!


**PUSH BUTTON STARTING**

positive, heavy-duty **electra glide type** with new 4-pole starter motor

Push the button . . . ZAP . . . and away you go. It's electrifying . . . it's unbelievable . . . it's new SPORTSTER H instant starting. Powerful 12 volt system, using a 32 ampere hour battery, leaps to your command to pulse SPORTSTER H's charging horses into action. Battery-oil tank combo is rubber mounted to isolate all vibration. Heavy duty system allows more power, too, for your favorite accessories. Make your fun more electrifying this year on a new SPORTSTER H.

*NEW SPORTSTER H ELECTRIFYING STYLING* — Stand back . . . take a look! Catch the sparkle of the new **twin tach-speedo** instrumentation. It's right up front where you can see it . . . but not the hidden drive cables. **New Headlight Nacelle** is really a beauty. An **Indicator Lamp Panel** is built right into the nacelle with aircraft design. New **Neat-Pleat All-Model Buddy Seat** has California styling that says "class" from the word go!

The electric starter appeared in 1966. Harley-Davidson introduced it on the Sportster Model H: "The hottest thing on two wheels!" Now all models had 10 to 15% greater power.

Photographed at world-famous Wisconsin Dells.

## SPORTSTER H BRIEF SPECIFICATIONS

**ENGINE — SPORTSTER XLH** — 55-cu.-in., air-cooled, four-stroke, V-type, twin-cylinder, overhead-valve engine. The size of the bore is 3". The length of the stroke is 3-13/16". Enclosed valve gear. Large intake valves. Low-expansion, special 9-to-1, high-dome, aluminum alloy, cam-ground pistons. Cylinder bores are honed. Cylinder heads with large intake port openings. Hi-Lift cams. Lightweight-racing-type tappets. Deep cylinder fins extend around exhaust ports for proper cooling. All main bearings retained roller type; double-tapered Timken bearings on the sprocket side; straight retained roller bearings on the gear side. Linkert carburetor.
**TRANSMISSION** — Harley-Davidson four-speed. Incorporated as an integral part of crankcase casting. Sliding dog clutches. Large, rugged gears for durability. Constant-mesh design. Foot shift, hand clutch.
**LUBRICATION** — Circulating lubrication system with gear-type pressure pump and gear-type scavenger pump. Transmission and front chain lubricated by oil supply separate from engine. All other bearings Alemite-Zerk fitted or prepacked.
**IGNITION** — Two-brush shunt, voltage-controlled generator; storage battery; spark coil; circuit breaker. Easy-starting and waterproof.
**CLUTCH** — Harley-Davidson multiple-disc. One-piece clutch discs. Left-hand-operated.
**DRIVE** — Motor to transmission by ⅜" pitch triple chain running in oil bath and sliding shoe tension control. ⅝" pitch, single-row roller chain to rear wheel.
**REAR SUSPENSION** — Swing-arm-type, sprung by means of two helical coil springs and controlled by means of two hydraulic, automotive-type shock absorbers, all enclosed in chrome covers. Pivot point of swinging arm is supported by pre-loaded Timken bearings.
**FRONT FORK** — Easy-riding hydraulic fork. Load is transmitted by long helical springs supported and contained in main tubes, hydraulically damped by oil of high-viscosity index. Hydraulic stops are provided in both recoil and cushion positions.
**TIRES** — Goodyear or Firestone, 3.50 x 18".
**BRAKES** — Fully enclosed front and rear brakes with molded anti-score lining. Front and rear brakes 8" in diameter and 1" wide.
**TANKS** — Extra-large, welded, heavy-gauge steel gas tanks with center filling cap. Capacity: 3¾ gals., including reserve. Reserve controlled by two-way gas valve with fuel strainer. Welded, heavy-gauge steel oil tank. Capacity: 3 quarts, with provision for filter. Oil tank cap has secure screw-down provision.
**FINISH** — Harmonizing two-tone color styling: Black, Pepper Red, Hi-Fi Blue, Hi-Fi Red or Hi-Fi Green with Birch White tank panel. See your Harley-Davidson dealer for other available colors and color combinations. Chrome and stainless steel trim.

## SPORTSTER CH SPECIAL SPECIFICATIONS

**ENGINE — SPORTSTER XLCH** — Same as the SPORTSTER H with the following features included: Fairbanks-Morse vertical magneto with standard SPORTSTER generator and voltage control regulator for horn and lighting.
**TRANSMISSION**—Harley-Davidson four-speed. Incorporated as an integral part of crank-case casting. Sliding dog clutches. Large, rugged gears for durability. Constant-mesh design. Foot shift, hand clutch.

High gear ratio — 1.00 to 1
3rd gear ratio — 1.38 to 1
2nd gear ratio — 1.83 to 1
Low gear ratio — 2.52 to 1

**TIRES** — Goodyear Grasshopper tread.
Front — 3.25-3.50 x 19 Rear — 4.00 x 18
**SADDLE** — Regular SPORTSTER type.

**SPROCKETS** — Overall ratio in high gear — 4.42 to 1
34-tooth engine sprocket
59-tooth clutch sprocket
20 tooth mainshaft sprocket
51-tooth rear wheel sprocket
**FENDERS** — Shortened front and rear fenders.
**GASOLINE TANK** — Capacity: 2¼ gallons.
**OIL TANK** — Capacity: 3 quarts.
**COLORS** — Available in all 1961 color combinations.

DM 4785.-- ab Freihafen Hamburg ,Zoll: DM 1126.--

GEORG SUCK
Kraftfahrzeuge
Hamburg Hagenbeckstr. 1

The Sportster H became a great success. This 900 had taken on a very European appearance, perhaps influenced by the Aermacchi, that now was a part of the Harley-Davidson Group.

1 FOR THE ROAD!

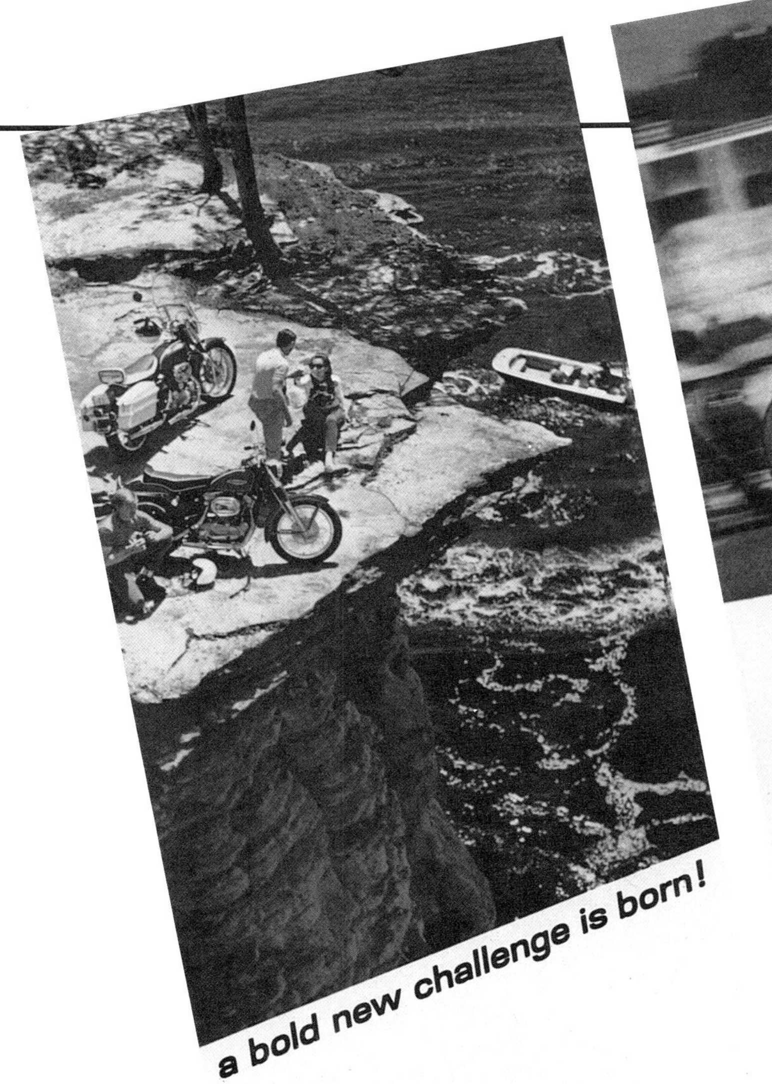

a bold new challenge is born!

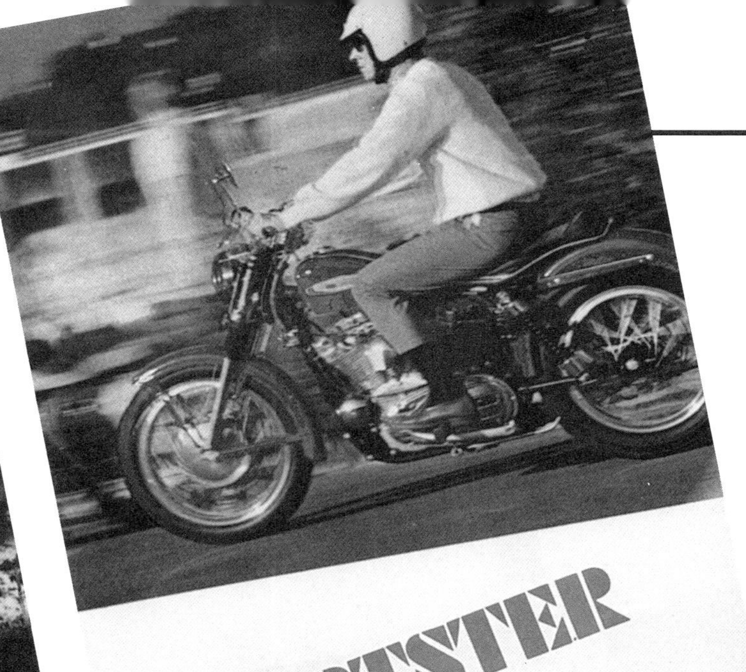

# SPORTSTER H & CH

**either way, you'll meet excitement face to face.**

Sportster. The road machine that's all snap. World's dragster record-holder. The kind of 900 cc power package that immediately takes charge of any situation. Quick. Confident. And explosive. Sportster's the kind of machine the others are still wishing they could put together. And after you've become familiar with its push-button electric starting, (XLH only), 12-volt power plant, and four-speed, constant-mesh box, you'll begin to wonder why they just don't give up trying. With Sportster on the scene, who stands a chance?

**ENGINE IMPROVEMENTS**— New case styling on both models. On XLH, elimination of starter pedal. On both, new Speedo drive for '68.

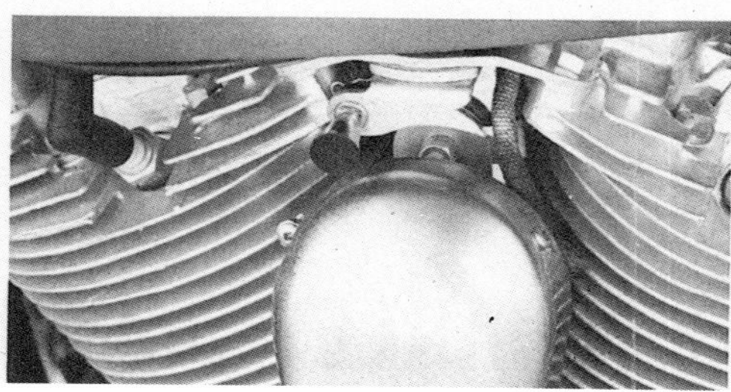

**SHOCK ABSORBERS**—Racing-type "shocks" were designed to give you the kind of road-hugging stability you need when the going gets tough.

**At right and left are more pages from the brochure whose title page appears on page 68. Among the innovations for 1968 were a new fork, changes to the motor housing and the shock absorbers. The motor produced 58 horsepower.**

# SPORTSTER H & CH when you're man enough to step up to some real two-fisted action.

Here's the one machine that really separates the men from the boys. Endless raw power for the most fierce excitement. Features a new speedometer to handle speeds up to 150 MPH, improved hydraulic front forks, and a new speedo drive shaft. How about it? Are you cut out to tame 900 cc's of hustle in the palm of your hand? If so, then there's only one more question. Will it be a Sportster H or CH?

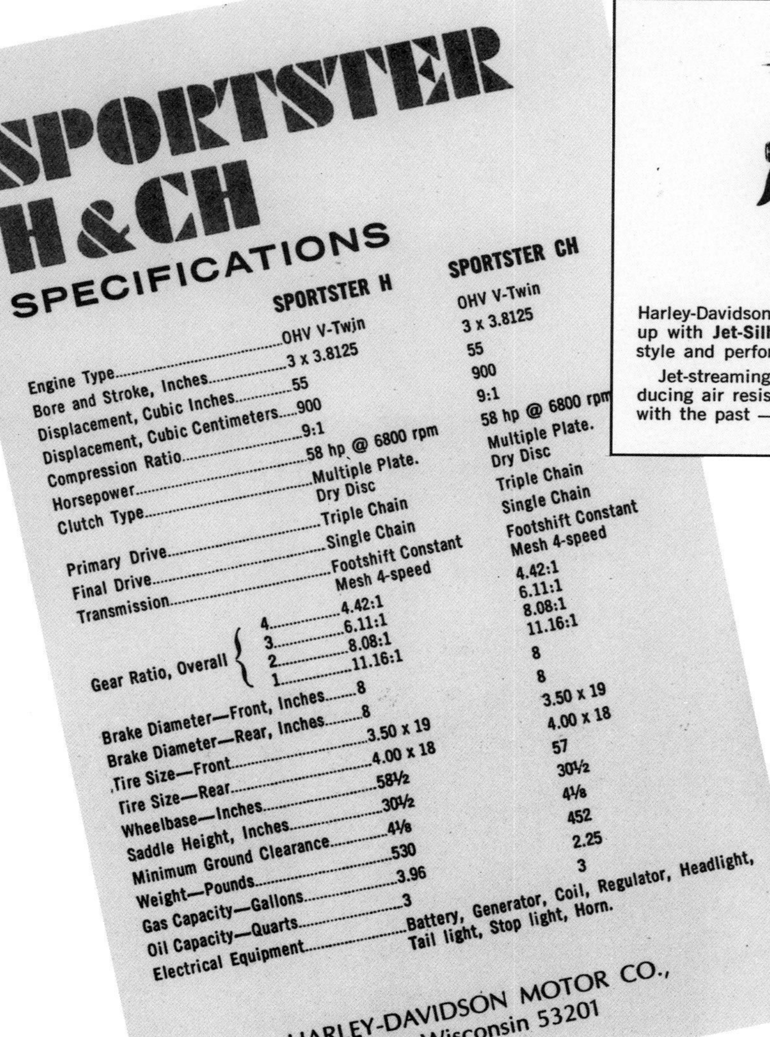

# SPORTSTER H & CH

## SPECIFICATIONS

| | SPORTSTER H | SPORTSTER CH |
|---|---|---|
| Engine Type | OHV V-Twin | OHV V-Twin |
| Bore and Stroke, Inches | 3 x 3.8125 | 3 x 3.8125 |
| Displacement, Cubic Inches | 55 | 55 |
| Displacement, Cubic Centimeters | 900 | 900 |
| Compression Ratio | 9:1 | 9:1 |
| Horsepower | 58 hp @ 6800 rpm | 58 hp @ 6800 rpm |
| Clutch Type | Multiple Plate. Dry Disc | Multiple Plate. Dry Disc |
| Primary Drive | Triple Chain | Triple Chain |
| Final Drive | Single Chain | Single Chain |
| Transmission | Footshift Constant Mesh 4-speed | Footshift Constant Mesh 4-speed |
| Gear Ratio, Overall 4 | 4.42:1 | 4.42:1 |
| Gear Ratio, Overall 3 | 6.11:1 | 6.11:1 |
| Gear Ratio, Overall 2 | 8.08:1 | 8.08:1 |
| Gear Ratio, Overall 1 | 11.16:1 | 11.16:1 |
| Brake Diameter—Front, Inches | 8 | 8 |
| Brake Diameter—Rear, Inches | 8 | 8 |
| Tire Size—Front | 3.50 x 19 | 3.50 x 19 |
| Tire Size—Rear | 4.00 x 18 | 4.00 x 18 |
| Wheelbase—Inches | 58½ | 57 |
| Saddle Height, Inches | 30½ | 30½ |
| Minimum Ground Clearance | 4⅛ | 4⅛ |
| Weight—Pounds | 530 | 452 |
| Gas Capacity—Gallons | 3.96 | 2.25 |
| Oil Capacity—Quarts | 3 | 3 |
| Electrical Equipment | Battery, Generator, Coil, Regulator, Headlight, Tail light, Stop light, Horn. | |

HARLEY-DAVIDSON MOTOR CO.,
Milwaukee, Wisconsin 53201

Harley-Davidson engineers took a page out of the latest jet aircraft design book . . . came up with **Jet-Silhouette.** It's a new lean and low look that hits a new high in motorcycle style and performance.

Jet-streaming lowers the center of gravity . . . gives you a new balance of power by reducing air resistance to an absolute minimum. And it's styling that makes a clean break with the past — **one** clean sweep from front fender to tail light.

**NEW DOUBLE-DUTY SEAT — Puts you low in the saddle!** Take to the road or ride in the rough — you can really lean into it on the Sportster's new double-duty seat. Straightline design, cradled between tank and fender, puts you at your ease for real down-to-earth riding pleasure.

**Puts you two in the saddle!** There is room for you — or **two.** Foam-rubber construction takes the bumps out of any rocky road ahead. However, if you're a bucket-seat man, conventional saddle is available as optional equipment.

The new seat bench was very atypical and influenced by European safety concepts. But the good old cowboy saddle with fringe and rivets just didn't look right on a sporting motorcycle!

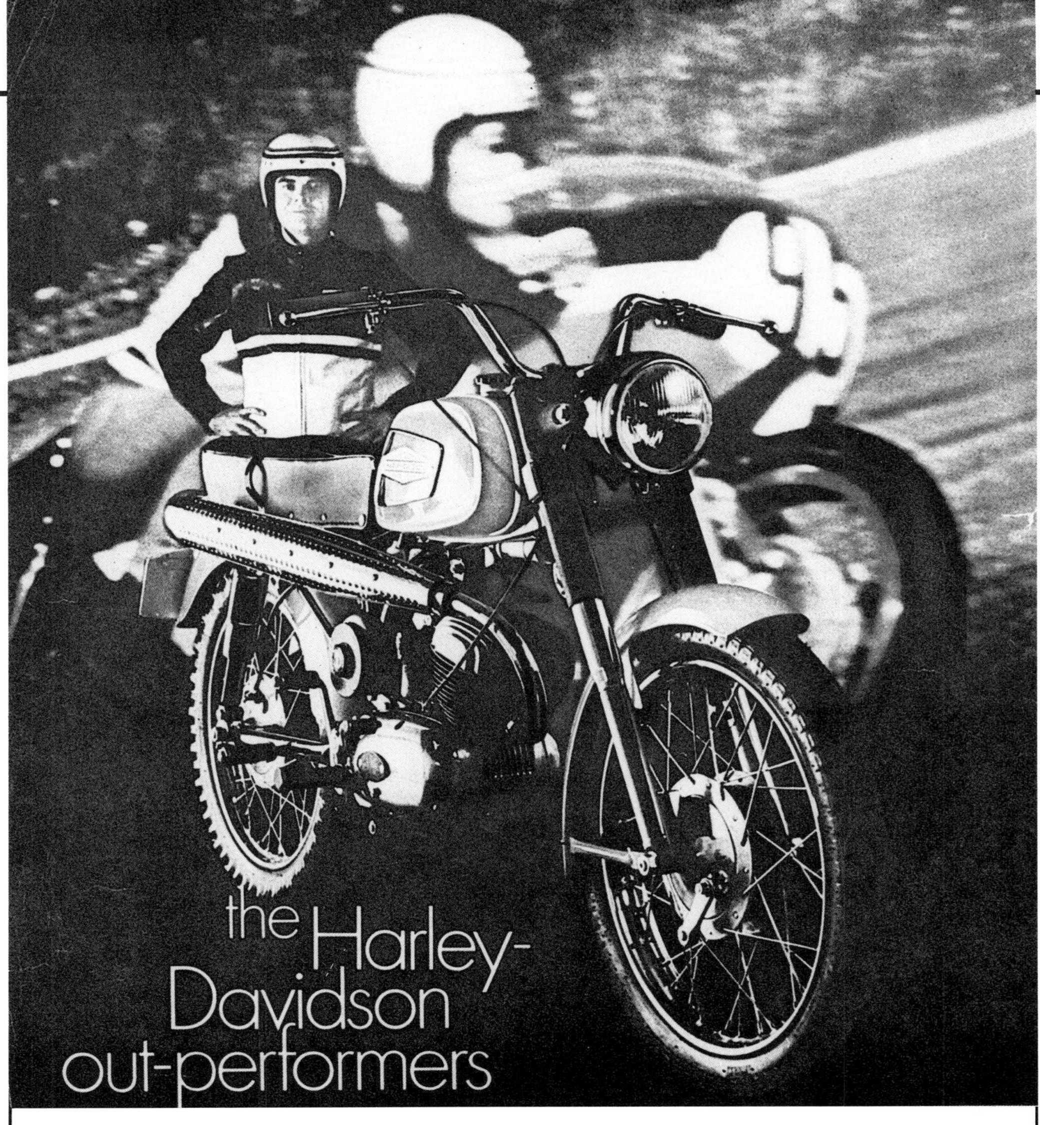


**The new Rapido explodes into 1969!** Here's a 125 cc stick of dynamite that weighs in with the 80's and 90's, but accelerates past the 175's. This year, Rapido comes in two models — a swinging street version and this hot new scrambler with high pipe, perforated heat shield, large sprocket and special off-the-road tire. Either way, Rapido will turn out the crowd and turn in the winning performance. Low end torque, wheelies and effortless top speed — $400 in the street version. This is the one they'll be talking about all year long. Get in on the conversation. Your Harley-Davidson dealer has the cycle, low-cost financing and insurance. Harley-Davidson Motor Co., Milwaukee, Wis.

...out-perform everything on two wheels.

An advertisement from 1969. A new model name appears: Rapido. Undoubtedly derived from the Harley-Aermacchi that came from Italy. The little 125 had grown to a 175cc machine. 1969 was also the year when the firm became part of the AMF Group.

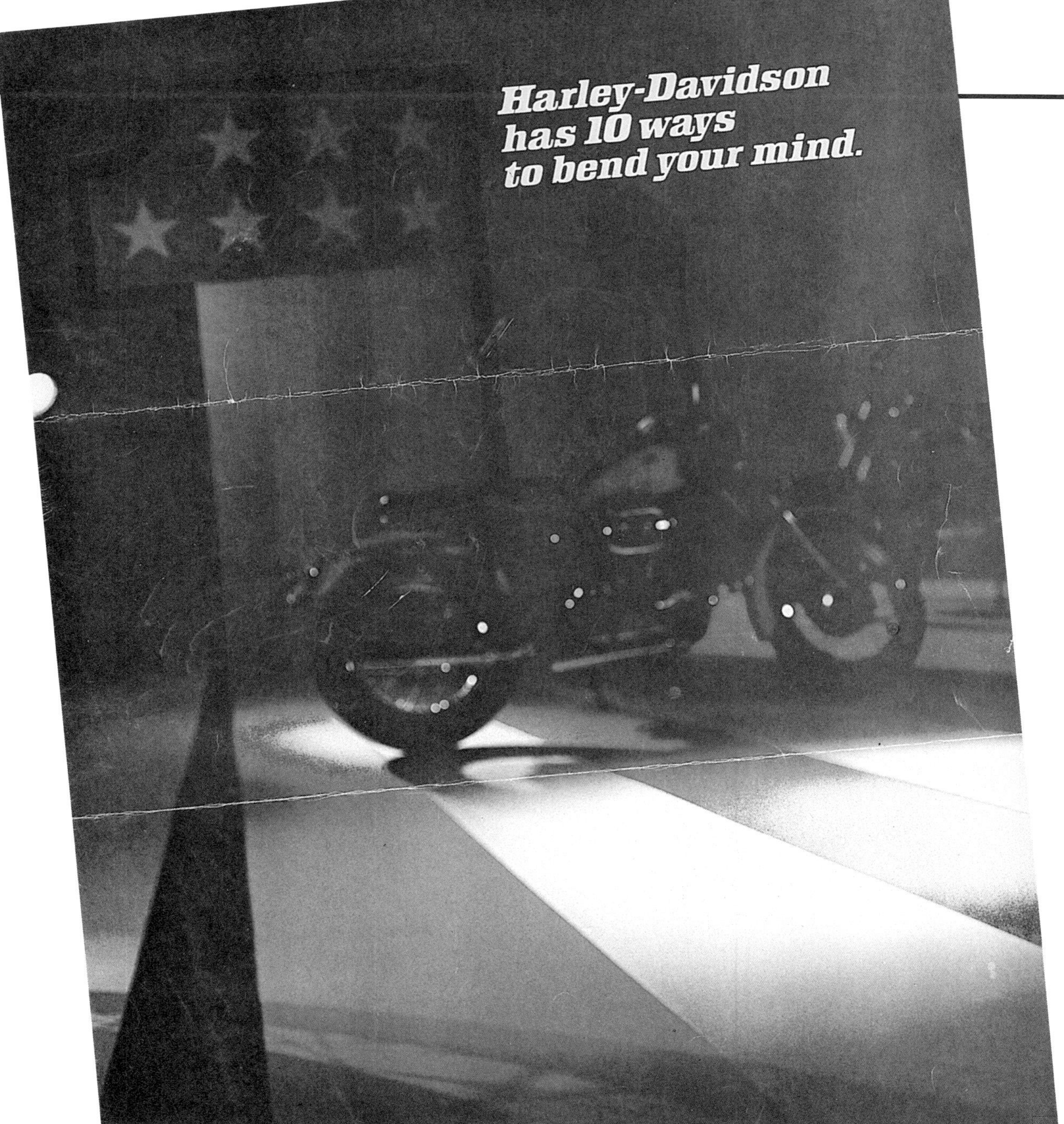
Harley-Davidson
has 10 ways
to bend your mind.

Title page of a brochure showing the 1971 models.

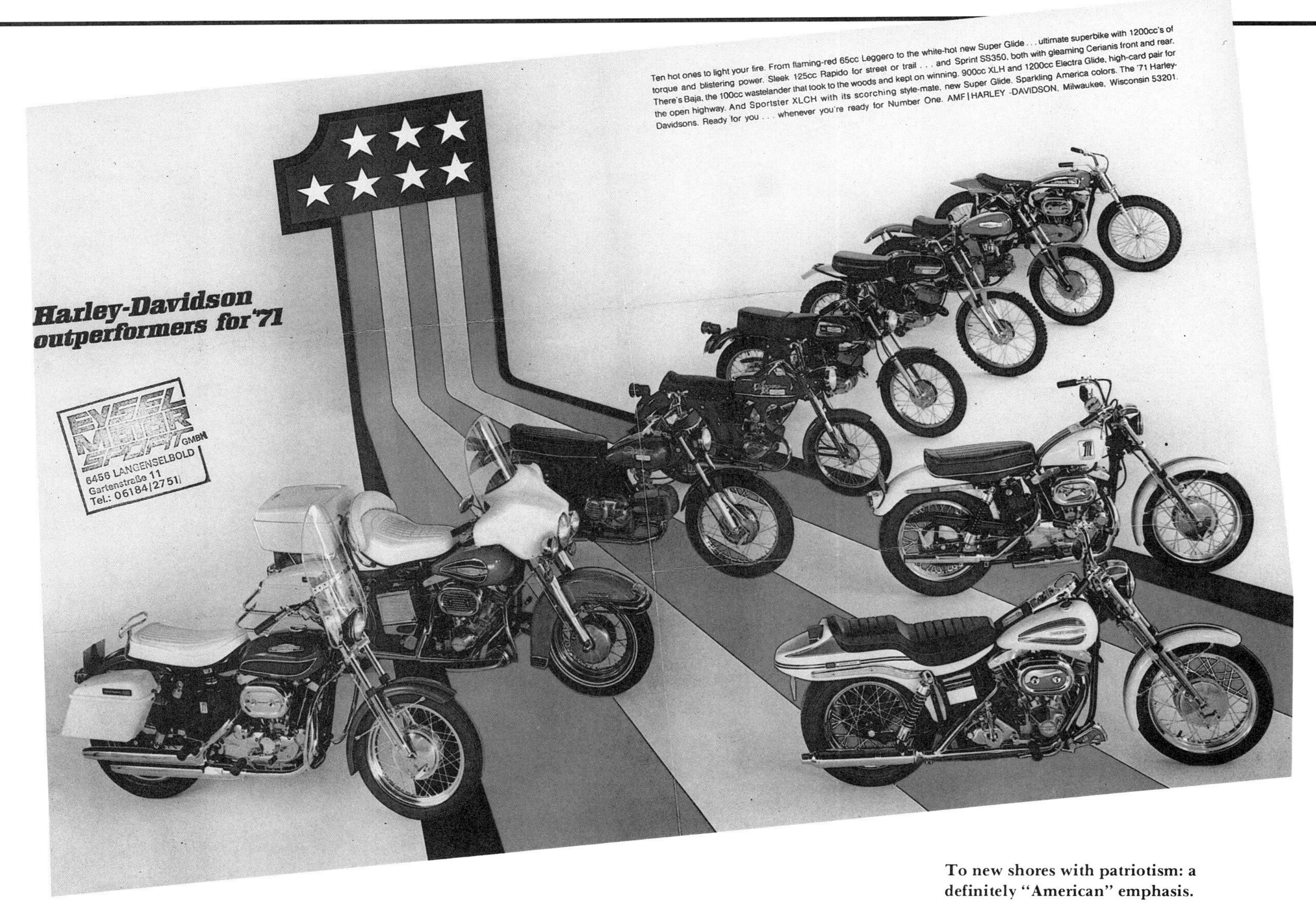

Ten hot ones to light your fire. From flaming-red 65cc Leggero to the white-hot new Super Glide . . . ultimate superbike with 1200cc's of torque and blistering power. Sleek 125cc Rapido for street or trail . . . and Sprint SS350, both with gleaming Cerianis front and rear. There's Baja, the 100cc wastelander that took to the woods and kept on winning. 900cc XLH and 1200cc Electra Glide, high-card pair for the open highway. And Sportster XLCH with its scorching style-mate, new Super Glide. Sparkling America colors. The '71 Harley-Davidsons. Ready for you . . . whenever you're ready for Number One. AMF | HARLEY -DAVIDSON, Milwaukee, Wisconsin 53201.
Harley-Davidson
outperformers for '71
GMBH
6456 LANGENSELBOLD
Gartenstraße 11
Tel.: 06184/2751


To new shores with patriotism: a definitely "American" emphasis. Harley-Davidson also had to deal with Japanese competition.

ELECTRA GLIDE. 1200cc OHV V-twin. 12-volt alternator. Bore, 3.437. Stroke, 3.969. 8:1 CR. Multi-plate dry clutch. 4-speed gearbox. Tires; 5.10 x 16 front and rear. Wheelbase, 61.5". 690 lbs.

SPORTSTER XLH. 900cc OHV V-twin. 12-volt system, electric starter. Bore, 3.00. Stroke, 3.81. 9:1 CR. Multi-plate wet clutch. 4-speed gearbox. Tires; 3.75 x 19 front, 4.25 x 18 rear. 4-gal tank. Wheelbase, 58.5". 508 lbs.

SPORTSTER XLCH. 900cc OHV V-twin. 12-volt electrics. Bore, 3.00. Stroke, 3.81. 9:1 CR. Multi-plate wet clutch. 4-speed gearbox. Tires; 3.75 x 19 front, 4.25 x 18 rear. 2.25-gal tank. Wheelbase, 58.5". 460 lbs.

XR 750 RACER. 750cc OHV V-twin. Fairbanks-Morse magneto. Bore, 3.00. Stroke, 3.22. 9.5:1 CR. Multi-plate dry clutch. 4-speed gearbox. 4130 steel frame. Fiber glass tank, seat/fender unit. Tires; 4.00 x 19 front and rear. Ceriani fork, Girling shocks. 312 lbs dry.

SPRINT SS350. 350cc OHV single. Bore, 2.91. Stroke, 3.15. 9:1 CR. Multi-plate dry clutch. 4-speed gearbox. Tires; 3.25 x 19 front, 3.50 x 18 rear. Wheelbase, 53.75". 311 lbs.

SPRINT ERS. 350cc OHV single. 1/2-speed Bendix-Scintilla magneto. Bore, 2.91. Stroke, 3.15. 10.5:1 CR. Multi-plate dry clutch. 4-speed gearbox. Tires; 3.50 x 19 front, 4.00 x 18 rear. Wheelbase 54". 259 lbs.

RAPIDO. 125cc 2-stroke single. Bore, 2.21. Stroke, 1.97. 7.65:1 CR. Multi-plate wet clutch. 4-speed gearbox. Street and trail sprockets. Tires; 3.00 x 18 front, 3.50 x 18 rear. Wheelbase, 48". Ground clearance, 6.3". 211.5 lbs.

BAJA 100. 100cc 2-stroke single. Bore, 1.97. Stroke, 1.97. 9.5:1 CR. Multi-plate wet clutch. 5-speed gearbox. Tires; 3.00 x 21 front, 3.50 x 18 rear. Ground clearance, 11.7". Wheelbase, 51.2". 212 lbs.

LEGGERO. 65cc 2-stroke single. Bore, 1.732. Stroke, 1.654. 9:1 CR. Multi-plate wet clutch. 3-speed gearbox. Tires; 2.50 x 17 front and rear. Ground clearance, 5". Wheelbase, 44.8". 134.5 lbs.

Number One
where it counts...
on the road
and in the records.
HARLEY-DAVIDSON
SUPER GLIDE. 1200cc OHV V-twin. 12-volt alternator. Bore, 3.437. Stroke, 3.969. 8:1 CR. Multi-plate dry clutch. 4-speed gearbox. Tires; 3.75 x 19 front, 5.10 x 16 rear. Wheelbase, 62.75". 543 lbs.


The choice of models is great; Harley offers something for everyone — even a 100cc off-road machine (Baja), plus heavy 1200 types as always. The machines with horizontal cylinders have racy Italian lines.

Freedom on two wheels: The XT 125 Of 1973 and its friendly rival the SXT 125, particularly off-road, with five-speed transmission and sporting bodywork (right).

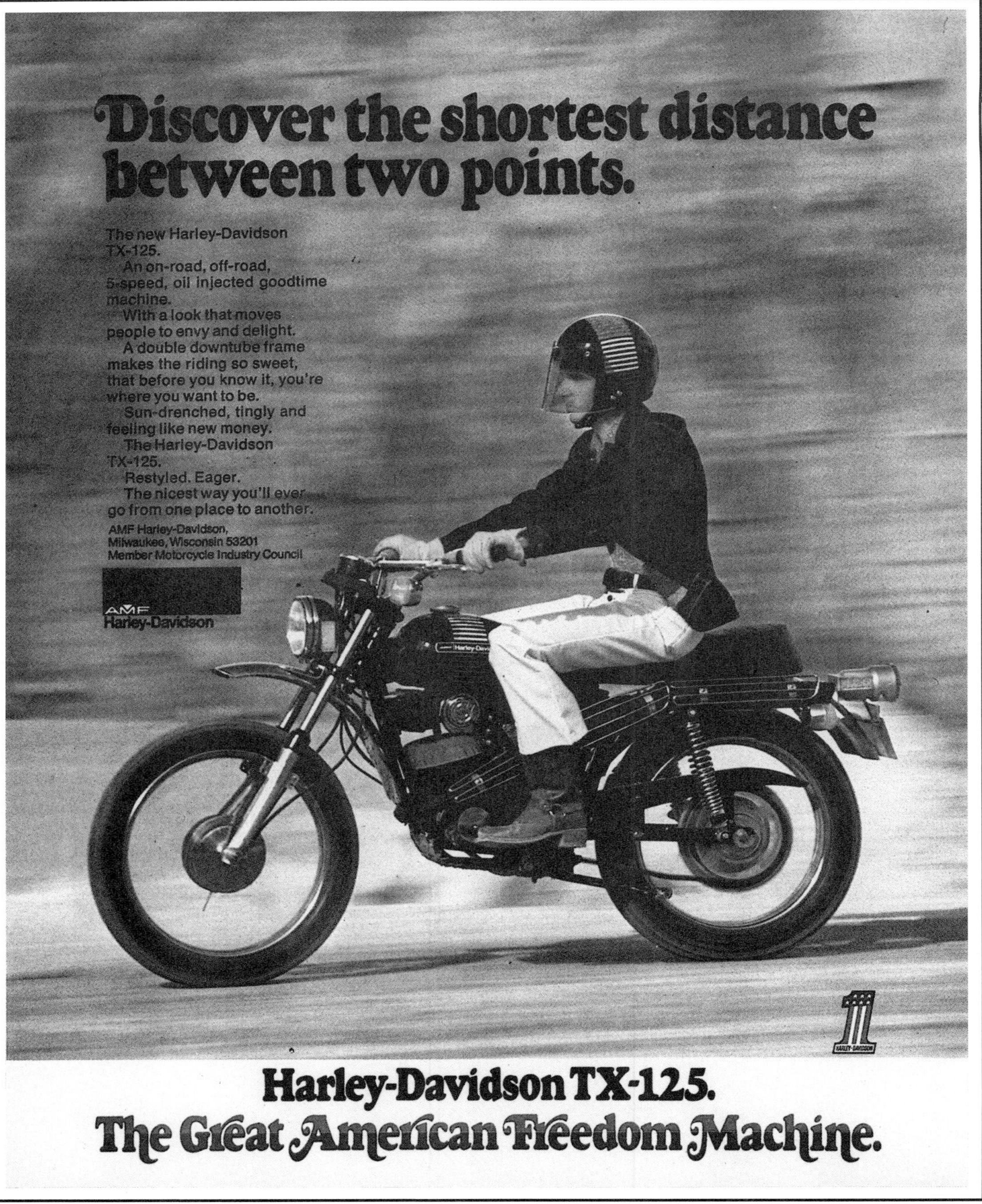

Discover the shortest distance between two points.
The new Harley-Davidson TX-125.
An on-road, off-road, 5-speed, oil injected goodtime machine.
With a look that moves people to envy and delight.
A double downtube frame makes the riding so sweet, that before you know it, you're where you want to be.
Sun-drenched, tingly and feeling like new money.
The Harley-Davidson TX-125.
Restyled. Eager.
The nicest way you'll ever go from one place to another.
AMF Harley-Davidson, Milwaukee, Wisconsin 53201
Member Motorcycle Industry Council
AMF
Harley-Davidson
Harley-Davidson TX-125.
The Great American Freedom Machine.

## SXT-125

The speedy two-stroke 125 in sporting form, here in a brochure for the British market.

# SXT-125

## Das Kraftbündel für Straße und Gelände!

Harley-Davidson hat die SXT 125 in bewährter Weise für zwei Funktionen gebaut: als Straßen- und als Geländemaschine. Das Resultat ist eine Maschine, die alle Baumerkmale ihrer "Großen Brüder" aufweist. Viele Bauteile sind die gleichen, wie bei der Harley-Davidson SX-250. Die SXT ist also keine aufgemöbelte 90er oder 100er – sie ist ein ganzes Motorrad!

Für einen so kleinen Hubraum ist die Leistung des Zweitakters mit automatischer Öleinspritzung einfach sagenhaft: Die Kraft des Motors läßt vergessen, dass "nur" 125 cc zur Verfügung stehen. Die SXT fühlt sich dennoch handlicher an, als die meisten 125er.

Dazu weist diese Maschine viele hervorragende technische Merkmale auf: schnelle und leichte Kettenspannung, wie bei Motocrossmaschinen; Sport-Vorderradgabel; dreifach verstellbare Federbeine hinten; automatischer Kettenspanner; Solid-State Zener Diode und Regler/Gleichrichter Elektrik; Fünfganggetriebe.

Und das ist noch nicht alles: Doppelrohrrahmen; verstellbarer Tageskilometerzähler; tiefer, gut gepolsterter Sattel; Bodenfreiheit von über 20 cm; wärmeableitende, verchromte Zylinderwand; Sicherheits-Reflektoren an beiden Seiten; Fußrasten für den Sozius; voll verstellbarer Scheinwerfer; Gummi-Schallabdämpfung für den Zylinder;

Sicherheits-Abstellschalter; großer Kraftstofftank für 10,5 Liter kraftstoffsparendes und sauberes 50:1 Gemisch.

Hervorragend auf der Straße – hervorragend im Gelände! Harley-Davidson bietet beides in einer großen 125er. Die SXT gewinnt, sie ist von Harley-Davidson.

### SXT 125

Technische Daten

| | |
|---|---|
| Motor | Zweitakt-Einzylinder |
| Bohrung und Hub | 56,13 × 50,04 mm |
| Hubraum | 123 ccm |
| Verdichtungsverhältnis | 10,8:1 |
| Kupplung | Mehrscheiben-Ölbadkupplung |
| Vergaser | Dell'Orto 27 mm Ø |
| Getriebe | 5-Gang |
| Gesamtübersetzungen | |
| 1. Gang | 29 |
| 2. Gang | 18,3 |
| 3. Gang | 13,2 |
| 4. Gang | 10,6 |
| 5. Gang | 8,5 |
| Hinterradfederung | dreifach verstellbar |
| Bremsen, vorn und hinten | 135 mm Ø |
| Luftfilter | Nassluftfilter |
| Kraftstoff-Füllmenge | ca. 10,5 liter |
| Reifengrösse, vorn | 3.00 × 19 |
| Reifengrösse, hinten | 3.50 × 18 |
| Radstand | 1359 mm |
| Bodenfreiheit | 218 mm |
| Gesamtlänge | 2080 mm |

- Fünfganggetriebe
- Automatische
- Öleinspritzung
- Dreifach verstellbare Federbeine
- Kettenspanner
- Doppelrohrrahmen

AMF Harley-Davidson

Technische Änderungen ohne Ankündigung vorbehalten. Weitere Informationen erhalten Sie gern von Ihrem Harley-Davidson Händler.

Printed in England

German version of the SXT brochure.

**SXT-125**
**The Power Pack for On or Off the Road!**

Harley-Davidson has built the SXT-125 in the time-tested manner for two functions: as a street and an off-road machine. The result is a machine that shows all the characteristics of its "big brothers." Many components are the same as those of the Harley-Davidson SX-250. The SXT is thus not an upgraded 90 or 100 — it is a complete motorcycle!

For such small displacement, the performance of the two-cycle motor with automatic oil injection is simply legendary: The motor's power lets you forget that "only" 125cc are there. The SXT, though, handles more lightly than most 125's.

Then too, this machine shows many outstanding technical features: quick and easy chain tension, as on motocross machines; sport-type front fork; three-way adjustable rear suspension; automatic chain spanner; solid-state Zener Diode and electric regulator/rectifier; five-speed gearbox.

And that is not all: Double-tube frames, adjustable daily odometer; deep, well-upholstered saddle; ground clearance of over 20 cm; heat-conducting chromed cylinder wall; safety reflectors on both sides; footrests for the passenger; fully adjustable headlight; rubber noise damping for the cylinder; safety stand; large fuel tank for 10.5 liters of energy-saving and clean fuel mixture.

Outstanding on the road — outstanding off the road! Harley-Davidson offers both in one great 125. The SXT wins; it is made by Harley-Davidson.

**SXT 125**

**Technical Data**

| | |
|---|---|
| Motor | Two-stroke one-cylinder |
| Bore and stroke | 56.13 x 50.04 mm |
| Displacement | 123cc |
| Compression ratio | 10.8:1 |
| Clutch | Multiple-plate oil-bath clutch |
| Carburetor | Dell'orto 27 mm diameter |
| Gearbox | 5-speed |
| Gear ratios: | |
| 1st gear | 29 |
| 2nd gear | 18.3 |
| 3rd gear | 13.2 |
| 4th gear | 10.6 |
| 5th gear | 8.5 |
| Rear suspension | Three-way adjustable |
| Front & rear brakes | 135 mm diameter |
| Air filterLiquid | |
| Fuel capacity | approx. 10.5 liters |
| Front tire size | 3.00 x 19 |
| Rear tire size | 3.50 x 18 |
| Wheelbase | 1359 mm |
| Ground clearance | 218 mm |
| Overall length | 2080 mm |

- Five-speed gearbox
- Automatic oil injection
- Three-way adjustable suspension
- Chain spanner
- Double-tube frame

AMF Harley-Davidson
Right to make technical changes without advance notice reserved. You can obtain further information from your Harley-Davidson dealer.

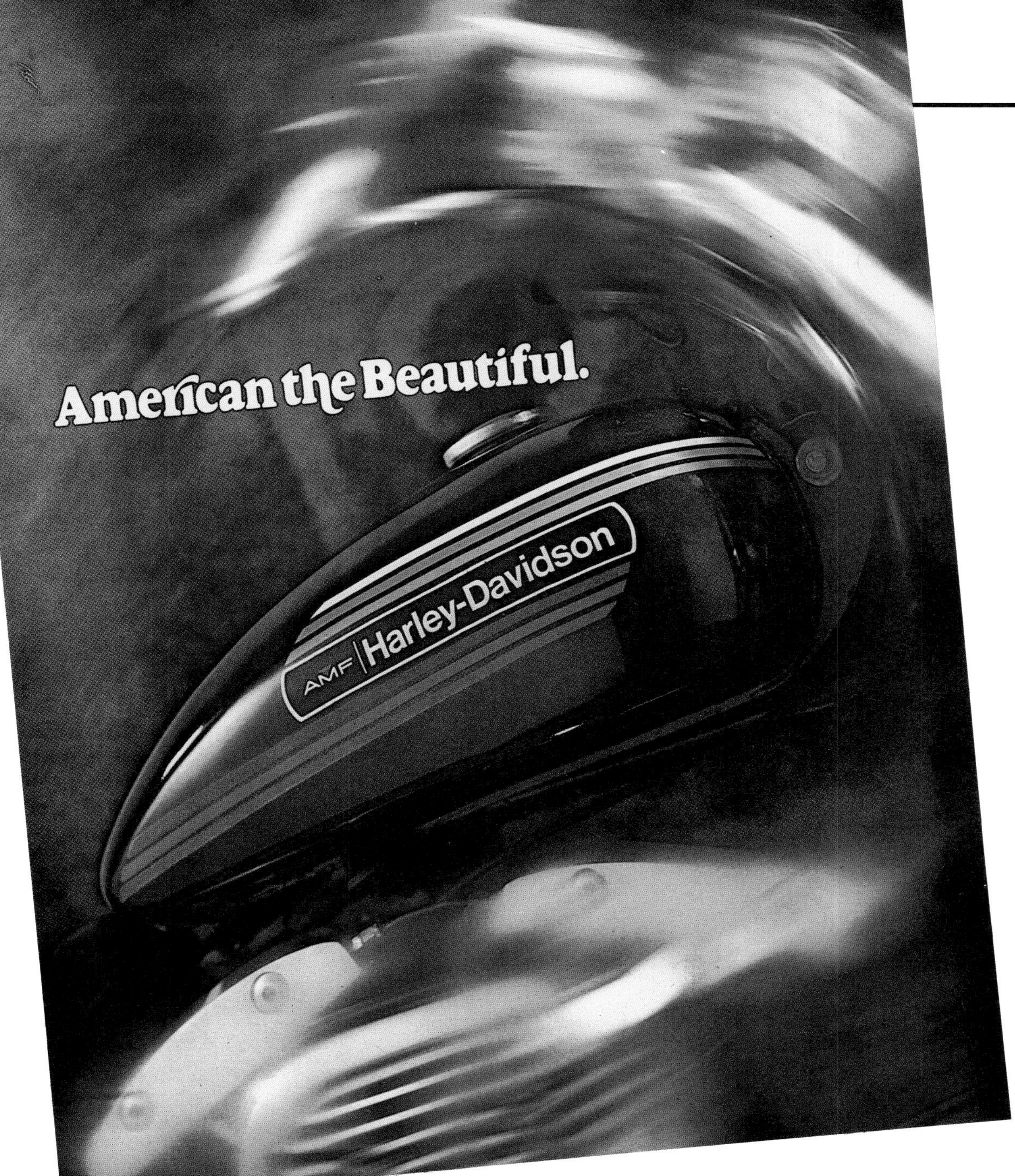


Patriotism here too in a brochure that came out in 1974. Ugly foreign competition?

**X·90** It's little but it has a big heart. A full 90cc two-stroke engine. With metered oil injection and a four-speed box. It also features fold down handle bars, spark arrestor muffler, new front fork, hydraulic rear shocks and true motorcycle suspension. Light enough to truck it to where you want to go. Then fire her up and go some more.

**Z·90** Double duty goodtime machine. Searches out freedom in town and out of town with an oil-injected, two-stroke single. It's got a four-speed trans, new aluminum brake hubs, rear shocks, turn signals and full electrics. Redesigned speedometer and mount, new front fork and brake, and smartly styled seat and tank rest on a sturdy double downtube frame. It's strong! And spark arresting muffler makes it quiet.

**SR·100** Brute Freedom! You gotta like hard riding and racing to appreciate the SR-100. Lighter and faster, carries an aluminum cylinder, two-stroke single. Five-speed trans, Ceriani front fork, new labyrinth-sealed brake hubs, 10.8" clearance, and you can see why it ran rough-shod over Mexico. And consistently wins in scrambles, moto-x and hare 'n' hounds. Tough dude, our SR-100.

**XL·1000** The twin of the XLCH-1000. But with a quicker way to get to freedom. Electric start. Otherwise, same four-stroke, V-twin power. New quick throttle and new racing-style, fade-resistant hydraulic disc brake, up front. All new "Security System" cycle alarm, load-variable rear shocks, speedometer, tachometer, beefier front fork and unitized handlebar controls including rocker-action safety switch.

**New SX-175** Here's our newest Freedom Cycle. A two-stroke single, oil-injected, chrome bore, aluminum cylinder, on-road, off-road machine; with a five-speed trans. It grooves up to eighty miles an hour. With adjustable rear shocks, tachometer, speedometer, breakerless CDI ignition, solid state regulator/rectifier, 12 volt alternator. It's got moto-cross type fork and labyrinth seal brake hubs. Our newest way to have freedom and fun!

**SX-125** Takes on city traffic or country trails. Powered by an aluminum cylinder, two-stroke single with metered oil injection. Put her thru her paces with a five-speed trans and ride in comfort with adjustable rear shocks. Solid state electronics, 12-volt alternator, turn signals and reset speedometer. Freedom, sweet freedom!

**SS-350** City slicker. And how! Rip-roarin' 350cc four-stroke power cycle. With a five-speed transmission, electric start and five-way adjustable rear shocks. Racing-style double leading shoe front brake. Double downtube frame for strength. Advanced muffler design for quiet. Plus speedometer, tach and turn signals. What a way to go! Why not take a friend?

**SX-350** Here's a jewel that'll flatten out country roads like they're city streets. Just touch it, and go. That's what electric start will do for you. A five-speed box and big 350cc engine will really carry you on to freedom. Naturally, turn signals, alternator are part of the deal. And all that freedom and grace are nestled on a double downtube frame. With crossbraced handlebars, five-way adjustable rear shocks and block trial tires. Ride on!

**FLH·1200** This is it! Nobody can take you higher! Because no one else has 74 cubes of power packed into a four-stroke, V-twin. It's always ready to run. Wherever freedom is. Without worries. It has a full-flow oil system, new "Security System" cycle alarm, 12-volt alternator, solid-state rectifier/regulator and exclusive fade-resistant hydraulic disc brakes, front and rear. Complete instrumentation is standard.

**XLCH·1000** You've got to be a man to handle this four-stroke, V-twin power cycle. We kid you not! On the street or in competition. It will roll! Rugged front fork, new quick throttle, new racing-style, fade-resistant hydraulic disc brake, up front. New "Security System" cycle alarm. Unitized handlebar switches including rocker-action safety switch. Traditional kick start tells you right from the beginning you've got a hell of a cycle.

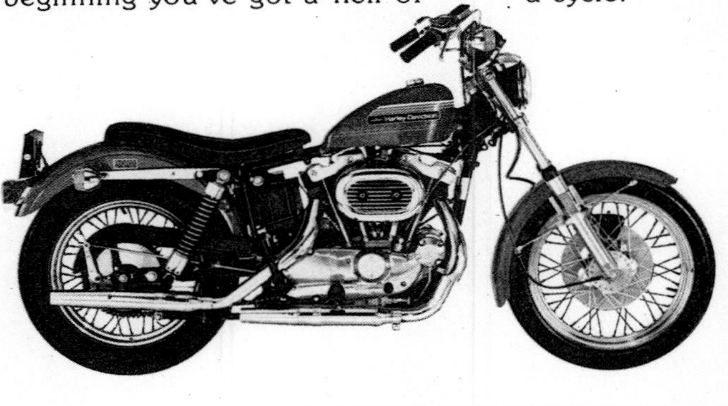

**New FXE·1200** A really sweet freedom ride. Fully instrumented with new electric start. Big, powerful...an ego trip if there ever was one. 1200cc performance makes this four-stroke, V-twin get up and go. New shift mechanism, big gas tank, dual exhaust system, speedometer, tachometer, new "Security System" cycle alarm and exclusive fade-resistant disc brakes, front and rear. The front brake is an all new racing-style brake. Also, safety rocker switch, new quick throttle control and heavy-duty front fork assembly.

**FX·1200** Another mind-blowing muscle machine. It's got all that great gear just like its twin brother, except for electric start. 1200cc power, four-stroke, V-twin, fully instrumented, speedometer and tach, new quick throttle control, new shift mechanism, new "Security System" cycle alarm and exclusive fade-resistant disc brakes, front and back. Front brake is an all new racing-style brake. This baby will roll!

# Where it counts, we're No. One.

**Number 1 Speed Record—set by Harley-Davidson.**

It happened in 1970. 265.492 mph! Our Cal Rayborn did it. With a specially-designed, V-twin overhead out on the Bonneville Salt Flats. Others have tried since. With three and four cylinder models. Even with two engines on one motorcycle. No record stands forever, but it's awfully nice to be first.

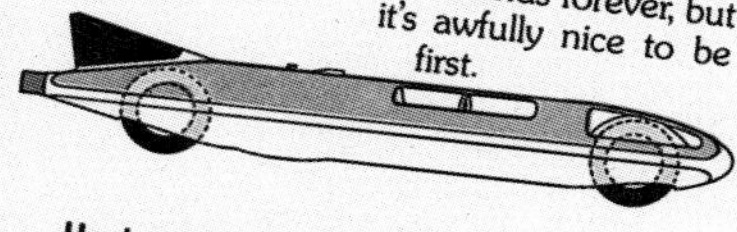

**Harley-Davidson. 1st to crack the 9-second, 1/4-mile barrier.**

Nobody could beat the long-standing 9-second record for the ¼-mile drag until Joe Smith came along. He did it on a Harley-Davidson V-twin. In 1971. He was clocked at 8.97 seconds (166.05 mph).

**Harley-Davidson. No. 1 A.M.A. for 1973.**

Harley-Davidson won the coveted A.M.A. Manufacturers Cup for '73. Top honors! Earned through team effort. Super riders. Machines built and maintained with integrity. Team spirit and pride. And engineering to back them up to beat out the best from every land. The very same combination of qualities that have made Harley-Davidson motorcycles outstanding for over 70 years. Every Harley-Davidson owner wins. Every time he rides.

**Harley-Davidson riders—Mark Brelsford 1973 A.M.A. Grand National Champion... Cal Rayborn, another No. 1.**

Unassuming Harley-Davidson team rider Mark Brelsford took the points, race after race, to win the coveted A.M.A. No. 1 plate for his bike. And the readers of **Motorcycle Weekly** awarded him another No. 1 when they voted him their Man of the Year.

The staff of **Cycle Magazine** chose another Harley-Davidson rider, Cal Rayborn, as their Rider of the Year. Because of his 3 firsts and 3 seconds in European racing, plus his many wins on home ground.

We can make the machines. But it takes a special kind of guy, like Mark and Cal, to make us look this great.

**Harley-Davidson. No. 1 Machine.**

The award came from **Motorcycle Weekly.** And the bike had to be the XR-750. The one on which Mark Brelsford blazed his way to the Grand National Championship. The one Scott Brelsford tamed to become Top Junior of the Year. XR-750. Undoubtedly the Machine of the Year. Winner more times than any other make.

**Harley-Davidson Dealers, wonderful guys to know.**

They're everywhere. Enthusiastically interested in you and your machine. They're motorcycle enthusiasts, they understand bikes. All of them. So, even if you're not fortunate enough to own a Harley-Davidson now, get to know our Dealers. They'll understand you. And they've got the factory-trained personnel and precision parts to keep your motorcycle going stronger, longer. Check them, too, for current hot accessories and clothing. They're much more than just another dealership.

They're Harley-Davidson Great American Freedom Headquarters. You'd better believe it.

**Harley-Davidson parts and service, 1st wherever you go.**

Replacement parts, identical with original Harley-Davidson components, are never farther away than your Harley-Davidson Dealer.

If you're a mechanical buff, enjoy working on your bike with our parts. But, if you're not, or if you need serious attention, the Harley-Davidson mechanic is the man to see. He's knowledgeable, factory-schooled. But the nicest thing about a Harley-Davidson is that it won't need much attention.

But drop in anyway and see what's new in motorcycling.

AMF Harley-Davidson
AMF Building
25-28 Old Burlington Street
London, W1X 2BA.

Harley-Davidson Motor Co., Inc. reserves the right to discontinue models or change specifications or designs at any time without notice and without incurring obligation. For more information, see your Harley-Davidson Dealer. AMF Harley-Davidson, AMF Building, 25-28 Old Burlington Street, London, W1X 2BA.

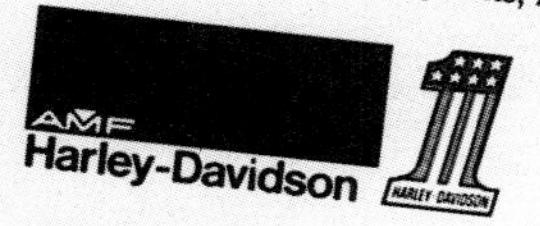


**The Great American Freedom Machines.**

PRINTED IN ENGLAND

**A brochure published for the British market in 1974. The English, by the way, had no particular love for American motorcycles.**

# Die Electra Glide FLH-1200

## Komfort auf Rädern, fast wie zuhause. Extras eingeschlossen.

Langstrecke und Zuladung sind zwei Begriffe mit besonderen Dimensionen. Die Harley-Davidson Konstrukteure haben das Problem konsequent durchdacht und das Ergebnis steht vor Ihnen: Electra Glide FLH 1200.

Der Motor hat – erneut im Detail verbessert – das fast schon legendäre Drehmoment, das bereits bei untersten Drehzahlen machtvoll einsetzt.

Der kraftstrotzende Zwei-Zylinder-V-Motor, die superstarke Hochleistungsfederung, die breiten Superreifen (übrigens mit hübscher Weißwand) und die mannigfachen Möglichkeiten, das Gepäck zu verstauen, sind die Komponenten, die bei der Electra Glide FLH 1200 den Transport von Mensch und Material zum Vergnügen machen.

Fahren heißt hier Fahrkomfort erleben. Nach wie vor ist unser Sattel * der einzige in der Motorradbranche, der durch Schraubenfedern und Stoßdämpfer gegen den Rahmen separiert ist. Es gibt eben keine Kompromisse, weder im Detail noch in der Gesamtkonzeption: Ihre Füße z.B. ruhen auf ordentlichen Trittbrettern und nicht wie anderswo auf den dünnen Sprossen einer Hühnerleiter.

Ein Fairing mit Windshield, seitliche Packtaschen mit Schutzrahmen und ein solider Gepäckträger zeigen unsere Art, eine Langstreckenmaschine zu konzepieren, zu bauen und zu verkaufen. Packen und abfahren, kein Stop beim Zubehörhändler.

Je weiter Sie von zu Hause weg sind, desto mehr wissen Sie die Feinheiten der Electra Glide 1200 zu schätzen. Die wartungsfreie und kontaktlose Zündanlage z.B. garantiert beste Starteigenschaften und einen hohen Ausnutzungsgrad des Kraftstoffes.

Der Langstreckenfahrer wird bei Harley-Davidson als besonders anspruchsvoller und wichtiger Kunde angesehen, jedes seiner Bedürfnisse soll durch eine totale, verpflichtende Auffassung von Konstruktionsprinzipien und sorgfältige Beachtung aller Details bedacht werden: Komfort und die Fähigkeit, genügend Ausrüstung mitzuführen. Dies ist der Grund, warum immer mehr Motorrad-Fahrer, nachdem sie sich das Angebot anderer Langstrecken-Maschinen angesehen haben, eine Harley-Davidson kaufen.

**FLH-1200**

Technische Daten

* Im Modelljahr 1979 ist auch ein am Rahmen montierter Tief-Sattel lieferbar (siehe Abbildung).

Reifengröße, vorn + hinten ...... MT90 × 16T
Radstand ...... 1550 mm
Sattelhöhe (separat gefedert) ...... 806 mm
Sattelhöhe (rahmenmontiert) ...... 711 mm
Bodenfreiheit ...... 118 mm
Gesamtlänge ...... 2362 mm
Motortyp ...... Zwei-Zylinder-V-Motor, OHV
Bohrung Hub ...... 87/101 mm
Hubraum ...... 1200 cm³
Drehmoment ...... 87.7 NM/3550 U/min
Verdichtungsverhältnis ...... 8 : 1
Vergaser ...... Ø 38 mm
Kupplung ...... Mehrscheiben-Trockenkupplung
Primärantrieb ...... Duplex-Kette
Sekundärantrieb ...... Kette
Getriebe ...... Viergang, Dauereingriff
Zündanlage ...... kontaktlos, elektronisch
Gesamtübersetzungen 1. Gang .. 10,74
2. Gang .. 6,50
3. Gang .. 4,39
4. Gang .. 3,75
Durchmesser der Bremsscheibe (vorn + hinten) ...... 254 mm
Kraftstofftank ...... 19 Liter
Öltank (Trockensumpfschmierung) ...... 3,78 Liter
Elektrische Anlage ...... 12 V
Lichtmaschine mit Regler/Gleichrichter, transistorisiert
Leergewicht ...... 326 Kg

MOTOR HARLEY-DAVIDSON CYCLES 1903 1978 75

AMF Harley-Davidson

Abgebildetes Modell zeigt US-Ausführung. Aufgrund gesetzlicher Bestimmungen anderer Länder sind Abweichungen möglich. Änderung von Ausstattung und Konstruktion ohne vorherige Bekanntgabe jederzeit vorbehalten. Weitere Informationen gibt Ihnen Ihr Harley-Davidson-Händler.

In 1978 Harley-Davidson celebrated its 75th anniversary. The Electra Glide was now expanded to 1340cc displacement (80 cubic inches). But the "small" models no longer existed; the one-cylinder types had been dropped from the program in favor of the twins.

**The Electra Glide FLH-1200**
**Comfort on wheels, almost like at home. Extras included.**

Distance and load are two concepts with particular dimensions. The Harley-Davidson designers have therefore thought the problem out thoroughly and the result stands before you: Electra Glide FLH-1200.

The motor — again improved in many ways — has the almost legendary torque that is already strong at low engine speeds.

The powerful two-cylinder V motor, the super-strong high-performance suspension, the wide super-tires (with nice whitewalls too), and the many possibilities for stowing luggage are the components that make transporting people and materials on the Electra Glide FLH-1200 a pleasure.

Here driving means experiencing driving comfort. As before, our saddle* is the only one in the motorcycle world that is separated from the frame by coil springs and shock absorbers. There just aren't any compromises, either in detail or in the whole concept: Your feet, for example, rest on proper footboards and not, as elsewhere, on the thin spokes of a "chicken ladder."

A fairing with windshield, side pockets with protective frames and a solid luggage carrier show our way of conceptualizing, building and selling a long-distance machine. Pack it and drive away; no need to stop at the accessory dealer's.

The farther from home you are, the more you are aware of the fine points of the Electra Glide 1200. The maintenance-free and contactless ignition system, for example, guarantees the best starting and a high degree of fuel utilization.

The long-distance traveler is regarded by Harley-Davidson as a particularly significant and important customer; each of his needs is to be met by a total, inclusive concept of design principles and careful consideration of all details: Comfort and the ability to carry enough equipment. That is the reason why more and more motorcycle riders, after they have seen what other long-range machines have to offer, buy a Harley-Davidson.

# The 1979 Electra Glide "Classic" with Sidecar

The unequalled prestige of riding a 1979 Electra Glide "Classic" can only be enhanced by showing off the enviable utmost in touring fun: The 1979 Electra Glide "Classic" with Sidecar.

Designed by Willie G. Davidson for availability as a complete vehicle unit, the 1979 limited edition Electra Glide "Classic" with Sidecar is Willie G.'s "piece de resistance" — for the die-hard tourist who *thought* he had everything. The two-tone tan and creme color scheme and hand-applied brown pinstriping which perfectly match the "Classic" are just the beginning. Willie G.'s eye for making the unusual dramatic insisted upon equipping the Sidecar with the same black cast mag wheel that you see on the "Classic".

You'll find other little details similarly rewarding, like the Sidecar drum brake, matching brown vinyl Sidecar bench seat and color coordinated snap-on tonneau cover.

Did Willie G. do it up right? We think it's a knock-out!

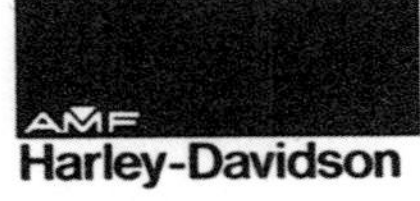


***Until you've been on a Harley-Davidson, you haven't been on a motorcycle.***

Subject to E.P.A. approval available 3-15-79.

Available now as before: The Harley with sidecar. The "boat" even had a slight similarity to those of the Thirties. This advertisement appeared in December of 1978.

# Harley-Davidson

## Der Rolls-Royce des kleinen Mannes!

MODELL 1928

MODELL 1928

GENERAL - VERTRETUNG FÜR OESTERREICH:

HARLEY-DAVIDSON-IMPORT-GESELLSCHAFT

HANS GROHE JR. & HUGO WINTER

TELEPHON 92-5-70, 98-1-11

WIEN, III. RENNWEG 46

GRÖSSTE SPEZIAL-REPARATUR-WERKSTÄTTE:
WIEN, III. ERDBERGERLÄNDE 30, TEL. 95-4-32

A look backward: Whether the English firm of Rolls-Royce agreed with the comparison? This advertisement appeared in Austria in 1928.

The Rolls-Royce of the common-man.

# Technical Data 1918-1978

With all its constancy of models, Harley-Davidson offered such a great number of type variations, especially after World War II, that it is scarcely possible to list them in the form of a chart in a small space. Thus the chart that follows lists only the most important main model series without attempting to be complete, while the specialized literature on the subject indicates sources of more specific information on technical data and differences in the models. It is not the purpose of this volume of the Schiffer Motor Chronicles to replace specialized literature on the Harley-Davidson.

| Model | B | C | E | F | J | FD | FDCA | FDCB | JE | JD |
|---|---|---|---|---|---|---|---|---|---|---|
| Years built | 1913-1918 | 1914-1918 | 1918 | 1918-1923 | 1918-1923 | 1921-1924 | 1924 | 1924 | 1924-1925 | 1924 |
| Cylinders | 1 | 1 | 2 | 2 | 2 | 2 | 2 | 2 | 2 | 2 |
| Bore x stroke, inches | 3 5/16 x 3 1/2 | | | | | 3 7/16 x 3 1/2 | | | 3 5/16 x 3 1/2 | 3 7/16 x 3 1/2 |
| Displacement | 494 cc, 30.17 ci | | | | | 1212 cc, 74 ci | | | 988 cc, 60.3 ci | |
| Horsepower | 4.34 | 4.34 | 8.68 | 8.68 | 8.68 | 9.5 | | | 8.68 | 9.5 |
| Ignition | Magneto | | | | | Magneto | | | Battery | |
| Gearbox | 1 speed | 2 speed | 1 speed | 3 speed | 3 speed | 3 speed | | | | |
| Drive | 1 chain | 1 chain | 2 chain | 2 chain | 2 chain | 2 chain | | | | |
| Notes | | 1918: 3 speed | | | | | Aluminum pistons | Steel pistons | | |

| Model | JDCA | JDCB | FE | FD | F | J | JD | A | AA | B |
|---|---|---|---|---|---|---|---|---|---|---|
| Years built | 1924 | 1924 | 1925 | 1926-1929 | 1926-1929 | 1926-1929 | 1926-1929 | 1926-1929 | 1926-1929 | 1926-1929 (1934) |
| Cylinders | 2 | | 2 | 2 | 2 | 2 sv | | 1 sv | 1 ohv | 1 sv |
| Bore x stroke, inches | 3 7/16 x 3 1/2 | | 3 5/16 x 3 1/2 | 3 7/16 x 3 1/2 | 3 5/16 x 3 1/2 | 3 5/16 x 3 1/2 | 3 7/16 x 3 1/2 | 2 7/8 x 3 1/4 | | |
| Displacement | 1212 cc, 74 ci | | 988 cc, 60.3 ci | 1212 cc, 784 ci | 988 cc, 60.3 ci | 988 cc, 60.3 ci | 1212 cc, 74 ci | 347 cc, 21.2 ci | | |
| Horsepower | 9.5 | | 8.68 | 9.5 | 8.68 | 8.68 | 9.5 | 3.31 | | |
| Ignition | Battery | | Magneto | Magneto | Magneto | Magneto | | Magneto | | |
| Gearbox | 3 speed | | | | | 3 speed | | | | |
| Drive | 2 chain | | | | | 2 chain | | 1 chain | | |
| Notes | Aluminum pistons | Steel pistons | | Steel pistons | Steel pistons | | | | Aluminum pistons | |

| Model | BA | JXL | DXL | JH | JDH | D | V 74 | D 45 | C 30 | B 21 |
|---|---|---|---|---|---|---|---|---|---|---|
| Years built | 1926-1929 | 1928-1929 | 1928-1929 | 1928-1929 | 1928-1929 | 1929 | 1930-1936 | 1929-1933 (1951) | 1929-1936 | 1934 |
| Cylinders | 1 ohv | 2 | 2 | 2 twin cam | 2 twin cam | 2 sv | 2 sv | 2 sv | 1 sv | 1 sv |
| Bore x stroke, inches | 2 7/8 x 3 1/2 | 3 5/16 x 3 1/2 | 3 7/16 x 3 1/2 | 3 5/16 x 3 1/2 | 3 7/16 x 3 1/2 | 2 3/4 x 3 13/16 | 3 7/16 x 3 1/2 | 2 3/4 x 3 13/16 | 3 1/32 x 4 | 2 7/8 x 3 1/4 |
| Displacement | 347 cc, 21.2 ci | 988 cc, 60.3 ci | 1212 cc, 74 ci | 988 cc, 60.3 ci | 1212 cc, 74 ci | 741 cc, 45.3 ci | 1212 cc, 74 ci | 741 cc, 45.3 ci | 500 cc, 30.5 ci | 347 cc, 21.2 ci |
| Horsepower | 3.31 | 8.68 | 9.5 | 8.68 | 9.5 | - | - | - | - | - |
| Ignition | Battery | Battery | Battery | Battery | Battery | Battery | | | | |
| Gearbox | 3 speed | | | | | 3 speed | | | | |
| Drive | 1 chain | 2 chain | | | | 2 chain | | | | |
| Notes | Aluminum piston | | | | | No official HP stated | Also VD, VDS, VLD | Also DL, DLD | CB with ohv motor | |

| Model | R 45 | VLH 80 | EL 61 | WL 45 | UL 74 | ULH 80 | F 74 | XA | S 125 | ST 165 |
|---|---|---|---|---|---|---|---|---|---|---|
| Years built | 1934-1936 | 1936-1945 | 1936-1952 | 1937-1951 | 1937-1948 | 1938-1941 | 1941-1978 | 1942-1945 | 1948-1952 | 1952-1957 |
| Cylinders | 2 | 2 sv | 2 ohv | 2 sv | 2 ohv | 2 ohv | 2 ohv | 2 Boxer | 1 Zweitakt | 1 Zweitakt |
| Bore x stroke, inches | 3 1/4 x 3 13/16 | 3 15/16 x 4 1/2 | 3 5/16 x 3 1/2 | 2 3/4 x 3 13/16 | 3 7/16 x 3 1/2 | 3 15/16 x 4 1/2 | 3 7/16 x 3 31/32 | 3 1/16 x 3 1/16 | - | - |
| Displacement | 744 cc, 45.3 ci | 1300 cc, 80 ci | 998 cc, 61 ci | 742 cc, 45.3 ci | 1212 cc, 74 ci | 1300 cc, 80 ci | 1212 cc, 74 ci | 740 cc, 45 ci | 125 cc, 7.5 ci | 165 cc |
| Horsepower | 48 | - | circa 40 | 30 | 40 | - | circa 40 | 7.5 | 3 | - |
| Ignition | Battery/Magneto | Battery | Battery | Battery | Battery | Battery | Battery | - | Battery | Battery |
| Gearbox | 3 speed (optionally 4 speed) | | 4 speed | 4 speed | | 3 speed | foot shifting as of 1960 | 4 speed | 2 speed | 3 speed |
| Drive | 2 chain | | 1 chain | 1 chain | | Chain | Chain | Staff | Chain | Chain |
| Notes | Also LR, LRD; followed by XR series | Also available with reverse gear | E series in EL, ES, ELS versions | W series in WL, WLD, WLDR; military versions: WLA and WLC | U series in UL, UHS, ULH, US versions | | F series in FL, FS, FLS, FLEF, FLHF, FLFB, FLB versions | Military cycles for Africa | | |

| Model | K 55 | Hummer | Sportster (X) | Super (X) | BT Super 10 | BT Pacer | Sprint | Rapido | XL 55 | ERS |
|---|---|---|---|---|---|---|---|---|---|---|
| Years built | 1953-1964 | 1955-1960 | 1958-1959 | 1960-1966 | 1960-1961 | 1962-1966 | 1962-1972 | 1968-1977 | 1963-1978 | 1969-1972 |
| Cylinders | 2 ohv | 1 Zweitakt | 2 ohv | 2 ohv | 1 Zweitakt | 1 Zweitakt | 1 | 1 Zweitakt | 2 ohv | 1 Zweitakt |
| Bore x stroke, inches | 3 x 3 15/16 | - | 3 x 3 13/16 | 3 x 3 13/16 | - | - | - | - | 3 x 3 13/16 | 2.2 x 1.91 |
| Displacement | 883 cc, 54 ci | 125 cc, 7.5 ci | 900 cc, 55 ci | 900 cc, 55 ci | 165 cc | 175 cc | 250 cc, 15 ci | 125 cc | 900 cc, 55 ci | 250 cc, 15 ci |
| Horsepower | circa 40 | 3 | circa 40 | circa 40 | 9 | 5 | 18 | - | - | - |
| Ignition | Magneto/Battery | | | | | | Battery | Battery | Battery | Magnet |
| Gearbox | 3 speed | 2 speed | 3 speed | 3 speed | 3 speed | 3 speed | 4 speed | 4 speed | 4 speed | 4 speed |
| Drive | Chain | Chain | Chain | Chain | Chain | Chain | Chain | Chain | Chain | Chain |
| Notes | K series in KR, KRTT, KRH, KH, KHK versions | Several versions: XL, XLH, XLCH | Several versions, followed by Sportster | BTU: 5 HP; also Scat and Ranger | Followed the BTU Super 10 | Also CRTT, C, H, SS, ERS | Also MLS | Several versions: also with magneto ignition: XLH, XLCH, XCT, XLCR | | |

Come over Spring Opening Week!
April 5th to 10th

Drop around Spring Opening Week. The latch string is out all day and every evening. Bring your pal along and join in on the good times.

With advertising cards and other giveaway articles, Harley-Davidson dealers have been advertising for years for meetings that they put on. Many motorcycle clubs in the USA grew out of activities sponsored by an involved dealership. The "bring a friend along" naturally meant nothing more than "get me new customers"!

There is a lot of Harley-Davidson literature, naturally most of it from the USA, some of which is also available in Europe. Here are a few examples, excluding the complete technical handbooks.

**The Harley-Davidson Cult** — A two-volume portrayal of the enthusiasm HD owners feel for their cycles. Author Gerald Foster has presented the nicest and most interesting photos, mostly taken in California, in these books. 128 pages each with about 120 photos.

**An American Legend.** This book is also by HD fan Gerald Foster. Here all series production models and racing Harley-Davidsons are presented and described in detail. The book includes 128 pages and some 80 pictures.

**Harley-Davidson im Bild** by Wolfgang Wiesner. More than a fascinating photo volume — an excellently written work of American motorcycle history with many interesting details. The book has 244 pages, 348 black-and-white and 70 color photos.

**Die Harley-Davidson: Mythos aus Chrom und Stahl.** This book, also by Wolfgang Wiesner, is very readable and includes history, technical data and typology. The book has 236 pages and 180 illustrations, one-third of them in color.

**Harley-Davidson — The Milwaukee Marvel** by Harry V. Sucher. This book is regarded in the USA as the standard work of HD history. Above all, it includes a detailed typology of all models from 1906 to 1988. 354 pages with 223 illustrations.

**The Harley-Davidson Motor Company.** David Wright wrote this book for the 80th anniversary of the firm. All production models with their data, many factory photos, 280 pages, 250 pages.

**Brooklands Series: Cycle World on Harley-Davidson.** There are now four volumes, covering 1962-68, 1968-78, 1978-83 and 1983-87. Each volume contains about 80 pages, with reprints of English and American motorcycle magazines. The quality of reproduction is very good. A4 format.

**Illustrated Harley-Davidson Buyers' Guide.** Allan Girdler wrote this "buyers' guide", which describes and basically evaluates all production models back to the 1936 model year. The book has 158 pages and 141 illustrations.

**The Big Book of Harley-Davidson** by Thomas C. Bolfert. A large compendium published under factory contract in 1989, with 462 pages of superb quality, particularly thanks to its large (24 x 32 cm) format and color photos throughout. The photos show every Harley-Davidson since 1903 in a contemporary milieu,plus the present-day models, the complete array of accessories and special tools. The Non-plus-ultra for the Harley fan.

Schiffer Automotive Series
MERCEDES-BENZ 190 SL 1955-63

# THE SCHIFFER AUTOMOTIVE SERIES

The **Schiffer Automotive Series** features specific models and automobile manufacturers in detailed discussions and pictorial format. Each volume presents a different history of the models chronologically to show their development. Color and black-and-white photographs demonstrate the production, testing, and road use of each automobile. Technical information, contemporary advertisements, cut-away views, and detailed charts of parts and statistics supply important information for owners, restorers, toy collectors, and model buuilders. Each volume contains a list of specialized collector clubs worldwide for the benefit of all.